In *Teaching Teachers: The Afrocentric Model of Education*, Professor Nah Dove's profound explication of the African episteme makes this cultural orientation available as an indispensable resource guide for educators not only to become more knowledgeable but also to recover our humanity. Grounded in the theory and practice of Afrocentricity, this book unerringly guides the reader through a critical historical, cultural, and spiritual reorientation that it is urgently needed.

Dr Joyce E. King

Benjamin E. Mays Endowed Chair,
Georgia State University

For the colonialists to impose themselves on Africans on the home continent and abroad, physical oppression attained through guns could not be guaranteed. Necessary to complete their project was Eurocentric education. Driven by this recognition, Nah Dove recognizes that flag and national independence in Africa, and bills of rights in the diaspora are not enough. Meaningful emancipation requires Afrocentric education, and that such a project cannot be realized without a deliberate programme of developing Afrocentric teachers. The task of an Afrocentric teacher is to re-educate, in the words of Carter G. Woodson, the mis-educated, and re-humanize the dehumanized.

Dr Simphiwe Sesanti

Institute of Post-School Studies, Faculty of Education,
University of the Western Cape (UWC), South Africa

Teaching Teachers: The Afrocentric Model of Education offers a comprehensive and inclusive step-by-step approach to centering the transfer of knowledge within an Afrocentric framework. This model has been thousands of years in the making. Dr Dove skillfully adds to this legacy by empowering the reader to build on these ancient foundations, offering a succinct, yet meticulous, step-by-step account to implementing this approach.

Dr Sally-Ann Ashton

Egyptologist, Psychologist, and independent scholar

TEACHING TEACHERS:
THE AFROCENTRIC MODEL
OF EDUCATION

Library of Congress Control Number: 2025912891

PRINT: ISBN: 978-1-942774-48-8
eBOOK: ISBN: 978-1-942774-49-5

Printed in the United States of America.

Mailing/Submissions:

Universal Write Publications, LLC
421 8th avenue, Suite 86
New York, NY 10116

Website: UWPBooks.com

This book has been partially supported with a financial grant from SAGE Publishing.

S Sage

TEACHING TEACHERS:
THE AFROCENTRIC MODEL
OF EDUCATION

Nah Dove, PhD

New York

Universal Write Publications

Universal Write Publications, LLC
New York, NY

Dedication

My mother Dorothy, my father Raymond, my brothers, Raymond, Gregory Adjua, Pierre, and my children, Siona Ankrah, Nadu, Ali Akintoye, Olatunji, Nadia Akua, Hope-Olani, my grandchildren, Adjowa, Abena, Kwabena, Nia, Rochelle, Otis, Des, Layla, Lani, my great grandchildren, Kymani and Kamiyah.

We are all the children of Africa, the mother of humanity and the resting place of our Ancestors (only the good may become our Ancestors).

I give praises and respect to those of every phenotype and gender, who try to live in Maat: Truth, Justice, Reciprocity, Righteousness, Harmony, Balance and Order, the foundation of civilization.

To the innocent lives lost through barbarism.

To those yet unborn.

To those who fight against all forms of oppression.

Table of Contents

Foreword

I remember climbing on top of the hill, looking at the numerous stone structures at Inzalo yelanga in Mpumalanga, the oldest human-made structure found so far, and wondering how I could not have known about this site. I knew many things about history and a few about what the teachers taught about prehistory, such as Stonehenge and the Minoan sites. Nah Dove's *Teaching Teachers* has entered the discourse of history and culture with a pedagogical instrument meant to assist other teachers and learners with understanding about humanity. This book is one that reveals erasures, shows concealments, and offers a platform for readers to use when trying to interpret what it is that we should be learning and teaching.

The scholar, Nah Dove, known for her insistence on clarity and precision, takes a delicate scalpel to the hidden layers of the racial falsification that stands at the entry to all Western disciplines. Others have talked about the misunderstandings that have been foisted upon the world by those who are disseminating a white racial supremacist doctrine in the so-called traditional disciplines of the West, and still others have made justifications for that dissemination, seeking to ensure that their careers are intact by supporting the most damnable parts of a distorted reality. Nah Dove is having no part of the petty tiptoeing around the real elephant in the disciplinary house; she is alerting all teachers and learners to the truth.

There are several pillars that she uses to build her house of hope for the future of pedagogy. This book, in some ways, accompanies her work called *The Afrocentric School*. I recommend readers to get that book to read alongside this one because this work, *Teaching Teachers*, is like a key to an understanding of why the author chose to include the information and activities that were put in *The Afrocentric School*. Of course, the brilliance of this duo is that one can read one without the other, such is the power and energy contained in both works, but it is very useful for teachers to be able to explain why certain things exist in the text.

No writer should assume that the reader, even if the reader is a teacher, will necessarily understand why things are placed where they are, why dates are important, why naming items, places, and things, as they have been named in the past is significant, or what role did economics, conflict, migration play in deciding and constructing culture. Well, Nah Dove does not assume we know and that is the genius of this work for the reader.

Dove's scalpel is used first to uncover the source of our problem with education in the West. She insists that there is only one humanity and that the construction of race has falsified humanity through categorization and essentially disrupted the normal order of community. Advancing an idea that a certain phenotype is superior or inferior prevents normal perception, behavior, or social interaction, hence insane. She does not scream this conclusion, but point-by-point demonstrates through the logic of science and rational thinking how the development of the ideology of white racial superiority has distorted how we teach as much as what we teach.

I am learning all over again, how I should view reality when examining concepts and events. She questions the idea of prehistory as being basically empty of human activity when one speaks of history and prehistory. Using what I call the period of culture formation, Mesuit, from the Kemetic root of birthing, she establishes the presence of human activity as far back as Inzalo yeelanga.

On every page of this book, there is something that is so refreshing in its vividity that it stays in the memory long after having read it. Europe, following the Arabs and the Brahmins, assigned itself the top place in a hierarchy meant to serve their patriarchy. As a reader or teacher, I am apt now to look at all instances of race and caste as being suspect because I am alert to the fact that they are concealing the source of their argument for or against other people. Dove has expertly pointed out that the nature of humanity exists without these categorical divisions meant to favor some and to disfavor others.

The book rivets the teacher and learner with insights into the rise of patriarchy and the decline in the matriarchy. No contemporary author has taken the work of Cheikh Anta Diop, the Per aa of African history and philosophy, so seriously as Nah Dove. If it is true as Diop insists that the two-cradle theory explains the conflicting realities in the world, then the fact that the southern cradle was matriarchy, meaning continuing the ideas and cultures that existed prior to the development of the more aggressive northern cradle, means that we have another way of viewing philosophies of the northern cradle; they are antithetical to the notions emerging out of the southern cradle.

Dove promotes for the reader–teacher the idea of Maaticity, that is the search for humanity based on seeking the principles of Maat in one's life. Almost no northern cradle ideology promotes this type of thinking because even where you have certain holy texts speaking of love everywhere those adherents exist, chaos appears. Seeking harmony and balance, based on truth, justice, righteousness, order, and reciprocity, leads toward the Maaticity that protects the rights of all humans, especially the oppressed.

Dove uses authoritative sources to buttress her arguments revealing the breadth of her reading and the depth of her understanding in presenting the instructive pedagogical context necessary to guard against being bewildered by Pan European Academy contradictions and hypocrisies. One can say that Dove has dismembered the reigning archetype of white racial supremacy by redefining the chronological chart of ancient history, exploring the residual impact of the false eugenic movement on academic disciplines, resisting the names introduced in the literature to defame, conceal, and hide African agency, for example, the use of Adam's Calendar for the ancient site known by Africans as Inzalo yelanga, the place of the rising sun.

The teacher–learner who reads this instructional work, based on solid philosophy and theory, will discover the remarkable advantage of having an Afrocentric guide that can be applied to many other books, events, and behaviors. Having this book will not only elevate your understanding of *The Afrocentric School*, but it will also make all readers, parents, homeschoolers, and thought leaders sharper in their analysis as it makes teachers more profound in their instructions. In this work, Nah Dove has raised the pedagogical bar for all Afrocentric-oriented scholars while simultaneously giving us the substance needed to scale all obstacles.

Dr Molefi Kete Asante

Founder of the Afrocentric Theory

Philosopher, Professor

Most Published African American Scholar with over 100 titles

Temple University

Acknowledgments

My life, and thus my works and ideas, have developed over the years through my experiences, and most importantly, the love and respect of those who have helped me live and survive. So many loved ones have passed. My family exists like an island of tranquility, with all its valleys and mountains, and fears and concerns, in a storm called life. My academic work is an expression of my life's experiences and learnings, set within theories, underpinned by teachings, some unexpected, shocking, sad, joyous, wonderful, and difficult, yet all necessary.

The academic world has produced some of the most wonderful scholars whose research, studies, theories, thoughts, activism have changed the world and influenced my own works as an African womanist seeker of truth. A major hope is to represent them respectfully and correctly. Like so many, I stand on the shoulders of Ancestors and Wisdom keepers; it would take a book to name them, some of whom I have met. In this current Afrocentric education book, people like Molefi Kete Asante, Cheikh Anta Diop, Asa Hilliard, Ivan Van Sertima, Ifi Amadiume, Mwalimu Shujaa, Wayne Chandler, Anthony Browder, Kimani Nehusi, George James, Chinweizu Ibekwe, Stephen J. Gould, Margaret Busby, David Olusoga, Maat Ka Re Monges, Sally-Ann Ashton and Augustine Agu, have been some of my great influencers.

Thank you, Dr. Ayo Sekai, founder and CEO of Universal Write Publications, a visionary publisher, scholar, and community builder, for transforming the literary and intellectual landscape through her trailblazing publishing house, dedicated to amplifying the work of some of the most brilliant scholars across the African Diaspora in academic research. Thank you, Geane dDe Lima, Sage Publishing, guru, for your support, incredible professional insights, and for your allyship and expertise. May my work amplify the vision of UWP Books and be a bridge to the next generation.

Introduction

As a result of my book, *The Afrocentric School [a blueprint]*, an interest arose in the idea of creating a book that interested teachers, schools, and homeschool parents could use to successfully teach Afrocentric education. *The Afrocentric School [a blueprint]*, in 2021, developed its pedagogy and syllabi based on a baseline study of "child upbringing practices" linked to the skills development of mainly rural nonliterate children living in West Africa. What I discovered was that we are all teachers and learners.

Most children lived in rural farming areas. The colonial schools were being built to suit the needs of the British and other European nongovernmental organizations (NGOs) whose powers, along with the government, dictated the use of lands and resources, with the inclusion of people's skills and particularly the erasure of indigenous institutions. Ethnographic research methods were of primary importance to creating policies and institutions to undermine indigenous ways deemed uncivilized or backward. Ghana's first installed African Prime Minister Kwame Nkrumah early Pan Africanist had called for a *United States of Africa* challenging the plans of the European and Arab colonizers across Africa. Conquerors tried to claim that they were African because they were born in Africa.

Essentially, it was the culture of Africa and the allegiance to African cultural beliefs that formed the bedrock for the choice of whether one has made the decision "to be African or not to be." UNICEF and the government were working toward the building of schools and training of teachers during the early 2000s when the study took place. The findings of the Afrocentric baseline study promoting the building rather than the erasure of indigenous institutions showed that the children were still cognizant of ecosystems, astrology, astronomy, mathematics, geometry, rhetoric, logic, music, and the arts. From this vantage, respect was given to the upliftment of these skills developed at certain ages.

Parents, particularly the mothers, were the source of data defining skill "development," synchronizing them with age ranges from pre-birth to 9 years was developed in the book up to age 15. It was noted that although the children were mainly nonliterate, their skills were advanced to literate children in the United States. Despite cultural colonial domination, they were still aware of their cultural identity, which is ironically the necessary outcome of education, to know who you are and thus one's mission. On the one hand, children had developed skills critical to maintaining and building upon ancient knowledge that had sustained their lives and environment.

On the other hand, literacy in the United States has undermined the development of cultural identity, based on the false information pro-pounded in institutions of "education" from nursery to university, underpinned by notions of who is human and who is not and who is civilized and who is not. These untruths manifest in social hierarchies and institutions that reify beliefs discriminating against and privileging people based on the amount of melanin in their skin, the darker the less intelli-gent more inferior, and gender, whereby the woman is deemed biologically and mentally inferior to the man. The findings relating to knowledge and skills were used in *The Afrocentric School* to enable parents, public school teachers, alternative school teachers, Black, African-centered and Afrocentric school teachers to use the book in relation to findings, from the skills and expectations of Black African children living in rural areas in Ghana rather than the findings of cognition, etc., from the Swiss edu-cational psychologist Jean Piaget who created ideas of cognitive development using his own three children as examples. The skills of the continental African children revealed their cognition in the manifestation of the skills that they exhibited in the tasks they accomplished and the knowledge that enabled them.

The Afrocentric objective was to create schools where these children lived that would facilitate and develop this knowledge in the creation of *Culturally Affirming Community Based Schools* (CACS) reflecting the community needs for everyone. African cultural orientation was viewed as ancient and brilliant, considering the major accomplishments that Africa had achieved. The children were viewed as recipients of this critical cul-tural knowledge, which was the foundation of their cognitive development.

It is in this light that I am writing a guide for teachers, schools, and home-schoolers to use the book with an understanding of building knowledge and syllabi based on the examples for each year of the child's skills development in the book. The concept of education in this book is grounded by the Ancient Egyptian (Kemetic) belief that education is the pursuit of self-knowledge and enlightenment and the understanding of cultural identity as proposed by Cheikh Anta Diop's two-cradle theory. Syllabi were developed in line with the skills of the nonliterate children. Diop recognized that the debasement and demonization of Africa was purposeful and culturally oriented, identifying the nature of the culture that would achieve this diabolical purpose and make it appear true. *Teaching Teachers: The Afrocentric Model of Education* is not limited to schoolteachers as it is a guide, not only for professional schoolteachers, but also to simply guide seekers of truth, with an understanding that from the Afrocentric vantage, we are all teachers and learners. There are pictures that relate to the information propounded, and terminology that is explanatory for a deeper awareness of some of the concepts used that refer to ancient African ideas.

BACKGROUND

This developmental model of Education is Afrocentric and grounded in the metatheory,[1] paradigm of Afrocentricity created by Molefi Kete Asante, who has written 110 books and is the father of the discipline of Africology. His metatheory will be explained more deeply further in the book. The book proposes that education is culturally oriented, in that the meaning of "education" is specific to the culture that develops it. A culture that debases a section or sections of its population to maintain certain social hierarchies of domination and privilege stands in opposition

---

[1]Asante, M. K. (1998). *The Afrocentric Idea: Revised and Expanded Edition.* Temple University Press. Asante asserts that "the significance of any metatheory is that it not only explains a given cluster of theories but also provides opportunities for enlarging human understanding generally" (p. 48). He explains his "desire to see a paradigm of complementarity that integrates discovery with verification where necessary" (p. 18).

to a culture that seeks egalitarian relations among its population. A culture built on hierarchy, for example, the supposed red people, the First Nations, indigenous people of the United States, the Blackest people captured and brought to the United States like animals, as enslaved people, women of all phenotypes, the poorest of all phenotypes, the mentally and physically disabled of all phenotypes, will create a different so-called education that is ultimately to maintain these disparities, maintaining those of the darkest hue at the bottom of each and every hierarchy. In this book, the significance of culture to human existence is highlighted offering a central theme throughout. One can go to Google or study culture from the discipline of anthropology, and it is generally defined through ethnographic studies that concretize the belief in race, whereby white societies are viewed as advanced and Black societies as primitive, relating to the cultures that formulate these societies, which is vehemently challenged in this book as a falsehood. For this work, the Afrocentric notion of culture is differentiated based on the values and beliefs of the creators of culture and life, that is the smallest unity of society, the woman and the man. Essentially, grounded in Cheikh Anta Diop's two-cradle theory, this book shows how culture determines the greatest differences among humanity.

The "mind" in this work is conceived from ancient texts as connected to the heart and soul, thus impacting on our thoughts and behaviors despite phenotypical differences in our looks and colors. Understanding the influence of culture on our minds, hearts and souls is critical to the work of this book in application to real life and death experiences. This Afrocentric educational model is culturally oriented, expressing ancient more egalitarian cultural values and beliefs ultimately adaptable to the needs of all pupils, teachers, and learners. It lays a framework for building ideas based on truths, uncovered in the research of Afrocentric thinkers, that can assist in the cognitive and psychological development of children as an aid to critical thinking, that is, logical thinking and cultural identity.

This book is designed with the intention to influence how the "teacher" can develop ideas, with the recognition that we are all teachers and learners, from the beginning to the end of physical life. What we know, from what we have learned, will guide what we teach and how we teach it. This Afrocentric perspective will, for example, enable the school-teacher to view new ways to develop curricula using the proposed Afrocentric Education model of thinking. Although the concept of education is seen to relate to both the academic discipline and schools, it is not limited to "schoolteachers" or "professors" who are carriers of the cultural orientation that they are taught in the discipline of Education, or through the Pan European Academy that creates hierarchies and privileges the racist, gendered, classes it embodies. Rather, this book embraces those interested in self-knowledge and teaching from the personal to the political in every academic discipline, as well as those with any interest in developing more egalitarian institutions from health care, the arts and politics to community centers, nurseries, social worker sites, hospitals, libraries, etc. In reference to the institutes of education, the current U.S. "education" model is based on the cultural beliefs of those who invented the United States.

Nearly a century ago, Carter G. Woodson (1933a, p. 4) warned us that, "the philosophy and ethics resulting for our educational system have justified slavery, peonage, segregation, and lynching. The oppressor has the right to kill the oppressed ... when you control a man's thinking you do not have to worry about his actions ... You do not need to send him to the back door. He will go without being told." His education makes it necessary. The Afrocentric model of Education, in contradiction to the U.S. model, which is based on the belief in the *races* of man, is grounded in the scientific knowledge that Africa is the birthplace of humanity and that there is one human race.

Moreover, if we humans go back far enough historically, we can remember and identify an ancient commonality culturally in Maat—the divine personification of Truth, Justice, Reciprocity, Righteousness, Harmony, Balance, and Order.

Importantly, it is argued that the notion of education is culturally oriented and thus to understand the U.S. notion of education, one must return to the history of how the United States was created, steeped in a culture that invented a belief in a hierarchy of humanity, based on color and gender through conquest, wars, domination, genocide, aggression in the taking of lands and wealth. The construction of the hierarchy of humanity, white supremacy, would become the foundation of the U.S. mindset ensconced in an unjust culture that would be taught as truth. The focus on the United States is to provide some of the contradictions of the so-called education that arise from the bloody establishment of a belief in *race—white supremacy* in the United States.

CHAPTER 1

The Root of U.S. "Education"

It was a pivotal moment in the history of the United States when a Black man, an African American born in Hawaii to a European American mother, Ann Dunham, and an African father, Barak Obama Sr., from Kenya, became the 44th President of the United States. Given the abhorrent and vile history of the capturing and enslavement of African people who were brought to the Americas—North, South, and Central by European enslavers and colonizers, it was almost inconceivable that a person who phenotypically represented the African type, connoting the historical and cultural legacy embodied in his color, would become president of the most powerful country in the world.[1] His parents had combined two supposed races, historically antithetical to each other, that in this fusion challenged the authenticity of his status as a Black man, an African American, and an American. Was he indeed an African American? Was he a Black man if his mother was white? Was he potentially a betrayer of Black Americans and/or a betrayer of white Americans since his mother married a Black man? What about all the other supposed races? Where did his allegiance lie? Issues of race arose regarding the body, behavior, and mind of the new president. What could we expect? President Obama's inauguration speech of 2009 stated:

---

[1]Phenotype is based on an ancient Greek word that relates primarily to how things appear, show, form, to our senses or consciousness. It has been used as a scientific concept to explain organisms and the external and internal complexities that manifest within environments. In terms of humanity, phenotype is underpinned by the reality that we are one human race, explaining that there are observable differences and traits in our physicality, which occur based on environmental factors, and other biological influences, thus physical features like melanin content in our skin, shapes of faces, and hair textures, etc., show differences that do not affect the similitude in being human beings regarding our human abilities and frailties.

Forty-four Americans have now taken the presidential oath. The words have been spoken during rising tides of prosperity and the still waters of peace. Yet, every so often, the oath is taken amidst gathering clouds of raging storms. At these moments, America has carried on not simply because of the skill or vision of those in high office, but because "we, the people, have remained faithful to the ideals of our forebears and true to our founding documents."

In this famous statement, the new president had in one sentence dismissed the history of the indigenous people, the First Nations people,[2] of the lands upon which this momentous history was taking place by viewing the "ideals of our forebears" as consistent with the founding of the United States and the Constitution, the laws of the lands, written by European racists whose forbearers had viewed African ancestors as less than human, only worthy of being property that could be abused and killed at the drop of a hat. The ancestors of the First Nations people were considered no better, and to some extent, their lives were deemed as less valuable than their lands (Dove, 1998a). However, although not prevalent, their enslavement (Reséndez, 2017) added value to their humanity. In concert with this reality, it can be said that overall, for enslaved African people, the chattel status gave primacy to their lives as an investment toward the building of the U.S. economy. There were many different nations in the Americas, North, South, and Central, and different "treatments" took place to dominate. Some First Nations people not enslaved, occupying in the flatlands were considered, merely at best, hunters (gatherers) living off buffalo that were purposely hunted and exterminated, leading to deaths of countless people of the First Nations (Thornton, 1987), land clearance, and the eventual importation of domesticated cattle. According to

---

[2]First Nations people is a definition chosen by the indigenous people of the Americas who may otherwise be known as Indians because of Christopher Columbus' mistake in thinking that he had sailed to the Indies and not to the Caribbean. Native American is another recognized term although the First Nations people viewed themselves as nations and not Americans. "Amerigo" Vespucci from Spain, travelled in 1497 to the lands of the First Nations people and knew, unlike Columbus, that he was not in the Indies. The lands were later called the Americas after his name and journeys. First Nations also applies to the original people of Australia who populated that land 70,000 years ago.

Thornton (p. 47), "[w]hile war and warfare and genocide were not very significant overall in the American Indian population decline, they were important causes of decline for particular tribes. Some American Indian peoples were even brought to extinction or the brink of extinction by warfare and genocide or, perhaps it is more accurate to say, by genocide in the name of war." Thornton elaborates on the prevalence of diseases which were the earliest killers brought to the people and the subsequent alcoholism, suicides, accidents, diabetes, and cirrhosis.

Owing to the death of Buffalo, ranchers would come to rely on the knowledge of enslaved Africans who had been cattle raising for thousands of years (Holloway, 1991, pp. 14–15). As it has been known and voiced by countless Africans and First Nations people whose cries for mercy were never heard, the "American Revolution" was a war fought to control the lands and wealth of the First Nations peoples by Europeans. The war was between the soldiers of the British colonies and the soldiers of the breakaway Europeans who wished to become independent from Britain. What was of ironic significance was that enslaved African people were asked to support both sides, either the British or the "Americans" who, as Europeans, were guilty of African enslavement. This is not unlike the current situation regarding the war being fought in the Sudan, whereby two groups of Islamic enslavers and conquerors of the indigenous Africans known as the Kush or Nubian Africans, hailing from an ancient civilization known as Ta Seti pre-ancient Egypt, are fighting without mercy over and for the beautiful ancestral sacred lands, that are bountiful and lush, of the Kush/Nubians as they have done for years. Some of these African people are Islamized and some Christianized and some retain their ancient African beliefs more ancient than the modern ones of Islam and Christianity.

Thus, President Obama's allegiance to the Eurocentric philosophy in his inaugural speech showed a reliance on a governing structure that was bereft policy-wise of humanitarian concerns for the indigenous people of the Americas as it was on Africans brought to the Americas who were captured and enslaved like animals, taken away from all that they loved dearly. Both peoples, affiliated with their nation groups, lost their lives and their worlds. This is not to say that President Obama was unable to become conscious of these racist disparities. He apologized to the First

Nations and tried hard to align himself with African American people who descended from enslavement. The point of the Afrocentric education model is that it is possible to change and become *conscious* not only of these mistakes but a developing awareness based on truth. As this work will show one can change, regarding the machinations of the cultural construction of race, and the significance of culture to transformation.

Following from the European wars for the domination of North American First Nation lands and leading to "independence," the American government soldiers fought the British soldiers of George III (1738–1820), whose marriage to a phenotypically light-skinned wife, Charlotte (1744–1818), from Germany in 1761, caused mayhem in racist Britain. History has shown that the Germans held dear, at one time, an African saint, Maurice, who died in 284 ACE. This may lead one to surmise that there was a time when the belief in race or the so-called race mixing was not considered the work of the devil. More current and probably equally worrisome for diehard racists in the UK is the marriage of Harry, son of King Charles III and his late wife Princess Diana, to Meghan Markle in 2018, a phenotypically light-skinned woman, daughter of Dora Ragland, of more recent African ancestry and Thomas Markle, of European ancestry in the United States. Ironically, George III married a woman who clearly had more classical Black African features from skin tone to hair, captured beautifully by the English painter Allan Ramsey.

Other painters depicted her as a white woman in the attempt to remove her from her obvious connection to her darker family and keep the family "white." One only needs to visit the Victoria and Albert Museum in

London to learn of dark skin African people in the European world in prominent positions. George III never owned or enslaved or entered the business of enslaving African people; in fact, he despised enslavement and was an abolitionist (Roberts, 2021, pp. 664–665) and married a Black woman. His royal family was responsible for the British who had gone to North America and stolen the lands of the First Nations people. The enslavement of African people from West Africa to the Caribbean had begun some 200 years earlier.[3] George III was influenced by his wife Charlotte, who banned sugar from the royal household, offered freedom from enslavement to those Africans, who became known as Black Loyalists, who fought to maintain the colonized lands for the British monarchy and, as a result, gained freedom.[4] This situation compromised the loyalties of enslaved Africans to two warring enslavers, as David Olusoga (2021) says:

---

[3]African people were transported from Sierra Leone by the British to the Caribbean from 1501 to 1641 according to the Colonial Williamsburg Foundation (https://slaveryandremembrance.org/articles/article/?id=A0116).

John Lok, a London merchant, traveled to Ghana in 1554, then the Gold Coast, and came back to England successfully, avoiding El Mina, the Portuguese fortress on the Ghanaian coast, where captured Africans were enslaved and shipped. John Lok secured 400 pounds of gold, pepper, and Ivory tusks along with "certain Black slaves," five altogether, whom he recruited to act as intermediaries and translators for further English expeditions. His "expedition" was the second after Thomas Wyndham's in 1553 which sought to challenge the Portuguese monopoly through plunder and trade. Wyndham, a seasoned pirate perished on his journey home. John Lok was the first English person to successfully challenge the Portuguese monopoly on trading and enslaving. He was the great, great, great, grandfather of John Locke (new derivation of the name, the enlightenment philosopher; Olusoga, 2021). The notorious John Hawkins, cousin of Frances Drake, later Sir, stole enslaved African people from the Portuguese, captured African people from Sierra Leone and took them to Hispaniola, today's Haiti, Ayiti, in 1562. His father William had sailed the coast of West Africa in the 1530s (Olusoga, 2021, pp. 50–51).

[4]In *The Book of Negroes* (2010, p. 479), by Lawrence Hill, a title borrowed from the original "*Book of Negroes*" that listed the Black Loyalists, there is a picture of a cartoon illustration of the time deriding Charlotte, George, and their family drinking tea with no sugar.

Those who fought for the patriots must have hoped that the ideals of the Declaration of Independence would, someday, apply to them, but more American slaves concluded that King George was likely to confirm their freedom than George Washington. Yet, while George Washington owned enslaved Africans, King George was monarch of a nation that, in the 1770s and 1780s, was the most prolific slave-trading power in the North Atlantic. That Britain, with her fleets of slave ships and her sugar islands carpeted with plantations, was regarded as the best friend of the slave, shows how desperately short of friends Africans in the New World were. (p. 150)

David Olusoga continues, "fifty-thousand enslaved Africans escaped and defected to the British. It was the first mass emancipation in the history of the North American colonies" (p. 151). He further notes that during this time, enslaved Black/African women and men escaped from George Washington, James Madison, and Thomas Jefferson, the author of the Declaration of Independence (p. 151). How ironic and contradictory, and yet it happened. One can say that George III betrayed racist ideals although he was the king of an enslaving, colonizing country. This situation is not unlike the conditions that African American soldiers fighting in wars representing the interests of the United States as a colonizing country, deeply consider, while being disrespected as Black women and men back home in the United States.

Black Canadian Lawrence Hill's (2009) research for his book, *The Book of Negroes*,[5] the fictional story of Aminata Diallo, a Black Loyalist of Nova Scotia, reveals 1,200 Black Loyalists who decided to board the ships back to Africa, Freetown in Sierra Leone. Hill further explicates that after the war of Independence, Sir Guy Carleton, commander-in-chief of the British Forces, carried out the terms of war and, in 1783, evacuated three thousand freed Africans to Nova Scotia, whose names were documented in the original, *Book of Negroes*, housed in the National Archives of London. On reading the original draft of the Constitution, Hill marveled at the contradictions of Thomas Jefferson's tirade against George III, while he himself owned

---

[5]This is a fictional story of Aminata Diallo linked to the story of Black Loyalists listed in the original *Book of Negroes*.

enslaved African people, and yet, some of his children were born from Sally Hemmings whom he also enslaved (pp. xi–xv).

The resulting victory against Britain led to the creation of the Declaration of Independence 1776 foundational to the formation of the American Constitutional operationalized by 1789. The Declaration of Independence was signed by 56 European men (American Council of Learned Societies, 1999), 41 of whom owned enslaved African people. These men are "affectionately" known as the Founding Fathers of the United States.[6] The signatory excluded anyone not representing their phenotype, gender, class, or sexuality (none of which we can be sure of). However, not everyone agreed, and some delegates did not sign. With the signing of this important document that could decide on the life and/or death of some of its population, the remarkable cultural history of the First Nations people prior to the conquests of the Americas was erased and replaced by a false history that ignored the humanity of the First Nations people and African people. How would the "new Americans" treat the indigenous people, and Africans brought from the continent? By 1789, the following Constitution of governing laws, prefaced by the falsehood of "we the people," was formerly ratified and ensconced within every institution from family, religion, education, healthcare, economics, science, politics, government, entertainment, to the arts etc.By deferring to the Constitution as bearing the ideals of "our ancestors" Barack Obama, our first African American President, a highly intellectual Black man, one of mixed or bicultural heritage, trained at Harvard, agreed to condoning the construction of a false history of the US. In doing so, he quelled the voices of the ancestors and descendants of those murdered in the taking of their lands and those murdered and stolen from Africa. In this way, President Obama supported the falsehood of the belief in race, that underpinned the behaviors and practices responsible for the planned genocide of the First Nations people and the inhuman enslavement of African people.

It is in this light I will argue that race is not real but a fabrication in an imagination ensconced within European and Southwest Asian cultures

---

[6]Thomas Jefferson, Robert Sherman, Benjamin Franklyn, Robert Livingston, John Adams are the five delegates associated with the development of the Constitution.

and philosophies, which assumes their own genetic, religious, and moral superiority, thereby creating beliefs in lesser beings, often viewed as brutes who will carry out orders on demand and be killed or punished if they disobey (Asante & Dove, 2021; Lindqvist, 1992).[7] One can transfer this type of racist belief to the western futuristic development of artificial intelligence (AI) as robotic, lesser beings with no spirit or feeling, programmed to obey orders with civility as they fulfill duties required. However, like anything, as conscious people, we can take AI and perhaps establish new ways to feed it knowledge that could produce ideas and analyses that cater to the truth-seekers' needs and that, if it is possible, they may detect truth-seekers' trajectory toward the betterment of humanity. The current beliefs have been and continue to be responsible for the hierarchy of humanity whereby humans are categorized into races from superior to inferior: the white man and woman (European) at the top, the yellow man and woman (Chinese) next, the red man and woman (First Nations), the brown man and woman (Malaysian, Arab, Indian), and the Black man and woman (African) at the bottom (Asante & Dove, 2021; Dove, 1998a; Gould, 1981). This arrangement is also gendered in that the man of every *race* is considered superior to the woman; however, in the unique case of the white woman, she is considered superior to every other man and woman in all the contrived races (Dove, 2018). It is incumbent on those who seek to "educate" to be acutely aware of this abhorrent situation, which seeks solutions from a false cultural foundation. To see things more clearly, one must step outside of the race paradigm. Clearly, one cannot step outside of the race paradigm if one is not even aware of its existence and that it is a falsehood (Dove, 2018). Understanding the nature of this "condition" will be a focus of this educational guide that may be used by educators: parents, students, teachers, readers, philosophers, and those interested, who may be from all walks of life and understand that we are all teachers and learners and there is no shame to either status and being both at the same time.

---

[7]Asante and Dove's *Being Human Being* is the quintessential reading for this work. Raoul Peck's documentary series with the same name as Lindqvist's *Exterminate all the Brutes* explores his friendship with Sven and the reality of the genocidal White Supremacist thoughts and behaviors with disregard of non-white humans during enslavement and colonization.

CHAPTER 2

Culture and Race: Effects on the Mind and Behavior

The scientific truth is that Africa is the birthplace of humanity and that all humans are genetically related to each other as one race: Humanity is the foundation of my argument. As humans, we are *Homo sapiens*. We are no different anatomically from *Homo sapiens* born 300 to 350,000 years ago. We have all been taught that humans arose from Africa. However, it is said that after humans left Africa, they divided into several races that became either advanced and civilized or inferiorized and barbaric. Even if the one race idea stays dominant, the civilization of humanity is racialized in the Eurocentric belief that as humans left Africa, lost their melanin, and became whiter, they became civilized. This idea was so powerful that there are many instances across the world where whitening became a policy among the darker skin so-called brutes, savages, and subhumans conquered by the so-called whites. This policy affected the First Nations people of the Americas and Australia and wherever they settled and developed their sacred lands.

Thus, the idea of whiteness and civilization and even living in colder climes are synchronized, and Greece becomes the fount of European (white) "civilization" although many Mediterranean people still show darker features because of their closeness to Africa. Ideas surrounding Greek phenotypes are rarely mentioned, but their affinity with Europe and whiteness is still taught as the foundation of human knowledge in European universities across the world in every country conquered. Those who continue to believe in the race theory or paradigm are related in thought to the pseudo-scientific belief in polygenesis, the idea that there are several races that arose in different parts of the world. This pseudo-scientific idea justifies hierarchical notions of human inferiority and superiority through the supposed existence of races arising in differing climatic conditions. White supremacists have used this belief to uplift their own humanity, believing that their lack of melanin in the skin denotes superior beings of high intellect, responsible for past great civilizations, as well as the current one, deemed the most superior of all civilizations. This belief has had a huge effect on dark skin individuals who use dangerous whitening creams to be considered; beautiful, intelligent, favored, respected, loved, cared for, as well as, to be able to reach higher positions in the race hierarchy, be less likely to be killed and hated, and be more easily employed, the list never ends. Even those considered white try to remove melanin spots that appear on their skin as they age. Fearful at the current time, that the *white race* is becoming extinct, there is a precedence on saving white people with the consideration for paying a $5,000 baby bonus to white women to have children to white men.

White men and their wives and families have successfully created university disciplines that have benefited in their development from the wealth accrued from the genocide of the original people of the lands in which they exist or have colonized, and the profit made from the labor of the bodies of those enslaved whom they have considered, and many continue to do so, as "brutes" or less than human. Since races are not scientifically real, it is possible to understand that the fear of white annihilation can be perceived as a mental illness. Asa Hilliard, an educational psychologist, Kemetologist, educationist, and multi-genius, proposed the idea in the 1980s that "racism is a mental illness, a disorder in the mental sense because it follows the rules of mental disorder, for example, manifestations of racist behavior as a result of domination, are the denial of reality, perceptual distortion, delusions of grandeur, phobias in the face of differences, and projecting blame by blaming the victims." These symptoms may be viewed as the outcome of the belief in the falsehood of race.[1] From this form of irrationality, the blame for the lack of white people,

---

[1] Please refer to Dr. Hilliard's video "Free Your Mind: Return to the Source," 1987, 6:00. https://www.youtube.com/watch?v=RQGU2TSToOA&t=659s, More recently, the work of Professor Joy DeGruy in her book *Post Traumatic Slave Syndrome: America's Legacy of Enduring Injury and Healing* (Uptone Press, 2005). Also, you may refer to the video for a talk in London by Joy DeGruy, https://www.youtube.com/watch?v=BGjSday7f_8&t=94s

will certainly fall upon the "white mother" who could be a light skin Black mother from a Black family, consciously Black but seen as white, who has children to dark skin men or not. The boundaries of race and color are not consistent and cannot be. In the race paradigm—white supremacy, a white mother is not trusted to be true to the white father. Indeed, all women are considered potential betrayers. The movement of white women to be with non-white men is considered a betrayal that maintains the idea that patriarchy is the only way to control women. This very modern thought can be linked to the ancient holy story relating to the first man Adam's wife Eve and Hawa, the first mother of creation, in the Hebraic, Christian, and the Islamic story, who commits adultery by fornicating with the devil, often depicted as Black and appearing as a serpent. It may be that subconsciously the black serpent represents the penis of the Black man that can taint the white race. Ironically, the serpent in Africa represented in ancient Egypt, Kemet, was not the feared vile reptilian creature it represents today to the followers of *race*, white supremacy. In Kemet, the serpent as cobra represented the mother protector of the people and sat on the crown of the Pharaoh, Per aa, whether female or male. The name Per aa, or the commonly used term Pharaoh is based upon *par'ōh* the Hebrew term for the Kemetic word Per aa, which means "great house." The major part of this guide is to establish the scientific truth of the African origin of humanity that all our ancestors are African and that we are all descended from Africa, and thus, we are essentially African people, phenotypically who have differences in our looks, hair textures, eye colors, skin colors, facial features and represent different features of *Homo sapiens*. There is a recognition in this work that many phenotypes exist that have been shaped and influenced by environmental experiences over time along with the knowledge that some dark Africans produce light skin or white Africans, some of whom are known to have albinism. People with Albinism are a rare and beautiful phenotypical example of humanity sometimes displaying the very classical Black/African features with little melanin in their skin, eyes, hair but as much melanin in their vital organs as all phenotypes. At the same time, some light skin mothers produce dark skin children. Moreover, all phenotypes are reflections of the original classical Black/African types from whom we are all descended. One must go beyond phenotype and race to recognize the significance of culture to our minds and behaviors because cultural orientation is the major differentiation among us that can be detected through our beliefs, actions, and behaviors.

Femi Biko, professor of Kemetology at Goldsmiths, London, has taught for years that Africa has different phenotypes, and thus, it was not only the migration out of Africa that changes occurred, but they existed in Africa prior to the early migrations, which we can date to beginning about 70,000 years ago. We become used to the idea that there is one phenotype that represents all continental African people and all First Nations people of the Americas, all Chinese people, all Indian people, etc., but this is not true; it is part of the construction of race and racism. Humans have always mixed, and changes have occurred through time, some Africans who left Africa came home and mixed again, after already mixing with others in different parts of the world. Essentially, we now live in a racist world that has placed false values upon differing phenotypes who have suffered the consequences of this falsity. The idea of this educational guidebook is to understand the significance of culture in our lives so that we may identify that there is a cultural construction of race and racism. This work will highlight how culture informs our minds and how our minds inform culture.

Afrocentricity, unlike other disciplines, recognizes cultural transmission as an avenue of connectivity among humans, whereby beliefs, values, behaviors, thoughts, historical knowledge, practices are transmitted intergenerationally over eons. There is also the recognition that attempts to prevent and stultify the process of cultural transmission of certain civilizations and societies, has been achieved as a major feature of colonization and enslavement. The cultural imposition of the conquerors' beliefs, values, behaviors has been violently foisted upon the victims so that they know only what the conqueror wishes them to know. In this way, without cultural knowledge, the foundation of cultural identity, and cultural unity, the oppressed are forced to understand a version of their humanity from the conquerors' vantage.

Africology focuses on African cultural beliefs and uses ancient Egypt, a Black African civilization that evinces the way people acted and produced knowledge that so many of us are unconscious of. The work of the Africologist is to help us relocate ourselves with our African heritage by awakening our cultural memory through knowledge—truth. An important question for seekers of knowledge, Afrocentric teachers, and learners is why we think the way that we do and ultimately how can we change some of the clearly unethical ways that we practice? Ethical ways can only be understood if there is a notion of unethical ways, and in this work, the ancient African moral principles of Maat—Truth, Justice, Reciprocity, Righteousness, Harmony, Balance, and Order—provide the framework for understanding what is ethical and thus the potential of becoming human and moving away from inhumanity (Asante & Dove, 2021). Maaticity is the process of becoming human following the principles of Maat. It is believed that by defining a notion of education, one based on truth of our human history, that is more fitting to our human needs, we may develop an understanding of our potential as a more global humanity recognizing our human mistakes and moving toward necessary change (Asante & Dove, 2021).[2] In effect, we would be returned to a time of sanity and, in that way, challenging the belief in evolution that has demonized those humans who came before, based on the ancient traditions that created the pathways toward betterment.

In consideration of the "legal" foundation of the United States and the whole notion of "education" and "educators," there have been questions regarding a system of schooling applicable to children of the United States. Information taught in schools has not successfully reflected the social realities that children face growing up in the United States that speak of "Democracy" and the equality of humanity and yet fails to put such ideas into action. Pedagogy and education have over time become more inclusive of recognizing marginalized groups that have been debased within the normalized hierarchies of race, gender, class, sexuality, disabilities whether mental, cognitive, physical, and age related, etc. This changing phase is owed largely to Black African leadership manifesting in uprisings, challenging to the forces of enslavement inclusive of unconscionable treatment, which, of course, did not end in the United States in the official year of 1865.

The indomitable spirit and energies of human rights fighters from as far back as the wars against the invading Hyksos, Persians (Iranians),

---

[2]Maaticity is a concept attributed to Nah Dove and developed in the book *Being Human Being* by M.K.A. Asante and Nah Dove regarding the principles and process of becoming human.

Assyrians, Greeks, Romans, and Arab enemies of Kemet, ancient Egypt, and the Kandake Queen leaders of Meroe in Kush, like Amanirenas, whose army in 10 BCE fought against Roman conquest and colonization and the 9th century 15 years' war of the Zanj in Iraq in Basra against their enslavement in the cruel salt mines. These historical and cultural struggles against enslavement and colonization can be linked to Denmark Vesey, Harriett Tubman, Nat Turner, Sojourner Truth, Frederick Douglass, Ida B. Wells, Steve Biko, Winnie Mandela, Robert Mangaliso Sobukwe, and countless others, some unknown, who continued the struggle for human rights later known as the Civil Rights and Black Power Movements in the United States. This was inspired by the anti-colonial movements in Africa that initiated the anti-apartheid movement in Azania (Simpson, 2023), and the Dalit movement in India against Brahminism/Hinduism (Asante & Dove, 2021; Dove, 2018; Rajshekar, 1987; Van Sertima & Rashidi, 1988).[3] These later African/Black struggles for human rights ranged from the 1950s to the 1970s, changed social conditions for everyone, challenging institutional structures and injustices, fundamental to maintaining social hierarchies in which Africans across Africa and African Americans to this day are still vulnerable to impoverishment, death, violence by police and governing authorities who support the racialization of humanity.

The Black Power Movement should be linked to the American Indian Movement (AIM), as both movements were integral to challenging the U.S. government (Churchill & Vander Wall, 1990). During the wars of centuries of stealing lands and attempts to deculturalize (Dove, 1998b), maintaining cultural integrity was necessary for First Nations people based on their ancient notion of human rights for the population. The forced migration to "homelands" or "reservations" in the style of the Brahmin and Christian religious beliefs of race, caste, and apartheid in South Africa–Azania, imposed to keep racial beliefs alive was one way in which some elements of culture could be maintained.

---

[3]Dalits are the "untouchables" in the Brahmin religion, commonly known as today's Hindu religion, whereby the race/caste hierarchy forbids each supposed caste/race to not interbreed. The progeny of interbreeding results in outcasts, no longer members of the religion who become less than human as debased and demonized beings.

At the same time, it should be noted that many of the indigenous people considered "red" were in fact Black in the race paradigm and African in the cultural paradigm because of their African matriarchal beliefs and values maintained within some of the earlier migrations out of Africa 70,000 years ago (Imhotep, 2021; McGhee, 2022). These beliefs still exist among First Nations people in the world and those original people of Australia who view themselves and their African matriarchal beliefs as at least 63,000 years old. These Africans who first populated the world outside of Africa were the first indigenous people in the world and the first Diaspora. In some cases, although phenotypes changed to accommodate environmental changes, there is evidence that some of the ancient African cultural beliefs remained with them.

Too often, those who decry specific social hierarchies are unaware that these hierarchies are all racialized, and theories pertaining to these hierarchies are often themselves racist. In this way, the most marginalized are often overlooked. For example, white feminists who theorize the dominance of patriarchy may raise issues pertaining to women, but not all women, some of whom may be non-white, dark-skinned, mothers, enslaved, unemployed, poor, trans, and disabled, etc. Moreover, some so-called white women may well be, as products and purveyors of patriarchy in the United States, collaborators in maintaining the structures of race and the privileges that they benefit from upheld by men, their fathers, sons, husbands, and lovers whom they see both as the "problem" and the solution. The inclusion of Black feminists into white feminism has changed the focus to care more deeply about women all over the world. The theoretical limitations of Black Feminist theory are that the intersections of race and patriarchy while true in the recognition of the debasement of Black women and men and in particular Black women, are firmly ensconced in the race paradigm invented by the theory of white supremacy embedded in the Pan European academy. Africology offers the theoretically grounded connection to our African cultural origins that existed in human history in its fullness to revere and respect the woman as the potential mother, thousands of years ago.

Africology allows the blame to exist in culture and not in men. In this way, both women and men become responsible for creating and developing more egalitarian cultural beliefs. Understanding African matriarchal culture offers a cultural objective that feminism does not, since its roots lie in Eurocentric academic philosophies. It may be said that their presence has been absent from many issues associated with patriarchy and the struggles of being not white that take place in the United States (e.g., police killings of Black women and men and the overrepresentation of Black women and men in prisons), inclusive of First Nations people (Goodwin, 2020a). Despite comprising roughly 6% of the U.S. population, Black women make up 22% of the women's incarcerated population. The U.S. incarcerates more women than any other nation in the world while mass incarceration, the drug war, and police violence are still viewed as a male problem, making women invisible within the criminal justice system (Goodwin, 2020b). In the class paradigm, the marginalized, unemployed poor are not even considered people; rather, they are considered the dregs of humanity and labeled lumpen or underclass; taxes are not spent to uplift these communities. The communities of the poor have been marginalized and criminalized for centuries in parts of Europe. Karl Marx defined the poor in England who became workers without enough money live, even when families and their children were working from dawn to dusk. For example, there is a preponderance of fentanyl and Xylazine users in the Kensington area of Philadelphia (SBC News, 2023), many of European heritage live with no help and no homes, and if they are African American and/or First Nations (phenotypically), these lives are considered as having even less value.Race is often excluded as foundational to the history of workers' rights. Enslaved African lives, blood and toil, created the profits that furnished the "industrial revolution" fashioned the rise of "working classes," across the European and Europeanizing world (Dove, 1995). African Americans as workers, whose ancestors died enslaved producing profit, have themselves struggled with the construction of race and racism within classes (Dove, 1995; Robinson, 1983). The Irish, many considered perhaps as lumpen, who were shipped to the Caribbean by the British colonizers waging wars; many against their will were enslaved and labeled *indentured servants*, and those sent to Barbados were called the "red legs." When it was convenient in the construction of "race," the Irish became white when previously considered less than human during the colonization of Ireland, which came in waves from the 1200s until their so-called independence in 1921. Still, the "Irish" now differentiated through political allegiances, religions, and land ownership would fight a complex civil war from the 1960s until 1998.

The Irish in the United Kingdom were disrespected during my childhood. My experience of growing up in London in the 60s reminds me of a time when rooms were for rent and notices put on the doors or in shop windows nearby stated: No Irish, No Blacks, No dogs or No Blacks, No Irish, No dogs. Irish captured, thrown on ships, sent to Barbados and named *redlegs*, and those sent to other islands in the Caribbean, when interviewed about their history, revealed that they were maltreated and enslaved (RetroGrading w/Phoenix*X, 2017).

The belief in the worthlessness of people not considered humans like the very poor in Britain was part of white supremacist thought, although they were white. Those white poor who attended schools were described by Cyril Burt, a Eugenicist and Educational school psychologist working for the London County Council from 1913 to 1940s who had control of thoughts regarding their futures, noted the physicality of the poor, said that their "features of inferiority as exceptionally prevalent in those whose faces are marked by developmental defects—by the round receding forehead, the protruding muzzle, the short upturned nose, the thickened lips which combine to give the slum child's profile a 'negroid' or almost simian (apelike) outline" (Burt, 1961, p. 12). Victims of societies that are inhuman toward others they deem less will be viewed from an Afrocentric cultural framework that employs a set of ethical standards from Africa by which we can make such judgments. From this vantage, the constructions of such beliefs are considered crimes against humanity, heinous, abominable, and culturally oriented. One can see the cultural similitude among these ideas. For instance, the Dalit of the Hindu system caste of Brahminism are considered "untouchables": This definition is not unlike the class-based belief that the impoverished people are "lumpen" or "underclass," subhuman, or subaltern (Ambedkar, 2022[1936]; Asante & Dove, 2021).[4]

What about the historical and cultural plight of the original people of the lands of the United States and those Africans conquered and enslaved and brought to the lands of the indigenous people? How was the wealth

---

[4]From the Latin "sub" meaning "below" and "alternus" meaning "all others."

acquired to even create a working class? In fact, the taking of lands from the First Nations people of the Americas, the reprehensible crimes committed, the genocide, the unconscionable criminality in taking ownership of all possessions, as if this was a righteous action ordained by the one true God, has to this day still not become an important question of ethics, morality, and economics as part of what should be learned at all schools, universities, and colleges (Chinweizu, 1975; Dove, 1998b; Thornton, 1990). Where are the "reparations" if any? Who should get them?

Race has so alienated and dislocated us from viewing each other as one humanity that we have African Americans who consider the United States to be their inheritance without regard for the people, our African ancestors who arrived here first 60 to 70,000 years ago whose lands were stolen and whose existence has been invisiblized. If the first Black/African American president has invisiblized the original people, how can we know? It shows that cultural domination is of the mind, heart, and soul; Eurocentric, cultural thoughts are embedded in our minds; and we have difficulty knowing who we are, or having a moral understanding of what the United States is to its people.

Ironically, in the early 1800s, prior to the official ending of enslavement in 1865,[5] in some parts of the United States, boarding schools for the First Nations children were developed by the U.S. government to force, under pain of death, the surviving First Nations families to lose their indigenous culture. Schools rose up to facilitate the idea of "civilizing the Indians." In 1879, Richard Pratt, school inspector of the notorious Carlisle Indian Industrial boarding school in Pennsylvania, claimed that such schools would successfully "kill the Indian in him to save the man." These schools were a method to force First Nations people, to lose their culture and accept the one being imposed. In this way, the children would lose their cultural values and view their treatment as necessary. Countless families and children lost their lives in this process in what can be called a schooling and not an educational process except if it can be viewed as becoming educated about the reality of land acquisition, cultural domination, and genocide.

---

[5]African enslavement did not end for another 50 years in the islands off the Georgia coast of the United States.

Mwalimu Shujaa (1998, p. 15) said that "[s]chooling is a process intended to perpetuate and maintain the society's existing power relations and the institutional structures that support those arrangements ... Education in contrast to schooling is the process of transmitting from one generation to the next knowledge of the values to the next knowledge of the values, aesthetics, spiritual beliefs, and all things that give a particular cultural orientation its uniqueness."

The land clearance of the indigenous people, the first Africans who arrived here, took place all over the Americas, as did their enslavement, while Black Africans were captured in millions, enslaved, brutally taken out of Africa away from all that was dear to them and brought to the Americas—North, South, and Central—and to the Arabian lands, as well as India. Countless African people died on the horrendous journeys through Africa and across the Atlantic and the Indian oceans. African people were not only taken out of Africa, but some also remained in Africa with their families destroyed and communities bereft of members vulnerable to the control of the invading and conquering armies of enslavers and colonizers that swept across the continent of Africa. Their goal was to take control of lands, resources, minerals, and the energies of the people to be exploited for uses other than in their own interests, whether to grow crops, mine gold, diamonds, copper, iron, steel, rubber, oils, medicines, coltan, uranium, precious stones like hematite, lapis lazuli, malachite, garnet, amethyst, diamonds, emeralds, tanzanite, and rubies..

We can see evidence of these crimes by just looking at a map of Africa and its divisions by Arabs and Europeans. The perpetrators of these atrocities against First Nations and African humanity were Europeans and Southwest Asian people, Arabs. There was very little difference in Euro-Arab objectives in the ways that land was stolen from indigenous Africans and indigenous First Nations people, a critical point made by Chinweizu Ibekwe (1975). In both cases, religions played critical roles in justifying abhorrent practices as godly or divine. Once culture is understood and included in analyses, it is possible to view these practices as cultural rather than genetically orchestrated.

This comparative analysis argues and shows that the race theory was formulated to place people into genetic type groupings based primarily on the melanin content of the skin and certain phenotypical features. It is problematic on many levels, from the spiritual and mental to the physical. The problematic assertion becomes more evident when those conquered become agents of the conquerors knowingly or unknowingly, regardless of phenotype, gender, sexuality, class, age, abilities, etc.

One can examine the case of the 44th President of the United States, who was born in Hawaii from a European mother and an African father. Having a Kenyan African father did not necessarily endear him to the nationalists of any color as he was not an African American in the sense that he did not suffer the history of enslavement specific to the North America experience. The history of the experiences of Africans on the continent captured, enslaved, taken away from their sacred lands, colonized by Arabs and Europeans, seemed relatively unconnected to that of African Americans. Africology sees this dislocation as problematic as the history of Black/Africans who remained on the continent is very pertinent to Africans who were enslaved and removed from the continent.

The intention of the enslavers was to break this cultural connection as part of colonization and cultural domination and furthermore to maintain this cultural dislocation, with the intention of creating a Black American unconscious of her, his, their, cultural connection, through a debased and uncivilized idea of Africa with an inflated idea of the "greatness" of the United States. In this way, African Americans and all other phenotypes would fear physical, cultural, and historical association with Africa, the supposed land of barbarians. In opposition to such ideas, Afrocentric theory brings together the notion of our cultural connections as a process of remembering self. For the United States, the Kenyan experiences and the murders of countless Kenyans during colonization and the Kikuyu *Mau Mau* fight toward Kenyan independence from Britain were unknown to many and, in that way, was of no consequence. By the usual standards of blackness based on melanin content, President Obama was a Black man and raised as one as well as experienced being one. However, the public, knowing that his mother was white, complicated the matter. He was now considered a "mixed-race" man, meaning he was the progeny of two supposed races. Thus, his genetic allegiance to either the Black or white side, as well as his ancestral experience, was brought into question at the time of his rise and even to this day, is/was he a betrayer of Black people or white people? Since his mission was to be the 44th President of the United States, his allegiance was to all Americans.

Considering the complexities of race as a belief, this teaching and learning guide will bring clarity into these dynamics and show how they have been used as excuses to regard some people as less than human and to endorse the genocide of some humans based on these beliefs. The belief in race as human differentiation has confused not only our understanding of our humanity but also erased our commonalities. Our differences are highlighted as genetic and thus insurmountable, and this cultural belief is ensconced in all U.S. institutions, including "education" from birth until our passing. I explain how using culture as a tool of analysis can create a theoretical framework for understanding how certain historical contradictions arise from miseducation (Woodson, 1933b) and become prevailing forms of cognitive dissonance that prevent the ability to "see" or understand truth.

Former U.S. President Barack Obama, a Black man, a bicultural man, a man of mixed culture, was culturally European American, grounded in the European "enlightenment" philosophical tradition and trained at Harvard. Thus, he believed that, by the statement at his inauguration, the ancient non-white histories that came before the Declaration of Independence, and the American Constitution, were irrelevant to the institutionalization of these documents that as laws proposed the falsity that they represented in the statement "we the people." This began a new era of modern fiction in a land called the United States led by an obviously Black President married to a beautiful African American woman with a degree in African American Studies and two beautiful daughters who complimented their family cohesion and complementarity, which could align with Maatic principles, challenging racist stereotypes. President Obama's overall governing national decisions produced some more caring policies, regarding the access of the poor, to health services, which is rapidly being undone by the current government that wants to go back to making life expendable in relation to the financial capacities. When the right to life is based on money, and some of us are purposely made redundant, based on how we look and the color of our skin, life chances diminish.

By understanding the significance of culture to the working of the mind and the development of thought and episteme: knowledge—truth, the guide can enable the creation of a curricula that can be more inclusive and embracive of the voices of marginalized communities. Marginalized communities refer to people left out of the history of humanity and the construction of the "laws" of the lands, embodied in the American Constitution. It is of significance to note again that religions oriented by the cultures that bore them have played pivotal roles in both creating and challenging these laws for and against marginalized people. For instance, the "Pro-slavery" movement was largely supported by religious ministers (Tise, 1987). The Quakers were against enslavement and their adherents were not allowed to own Africans ("Quakers and Slavery," n.d.). My pedagogical foundation is not religiously based, but it is ethical in that it is based upon the ancient principles of Maat that existed in Africa and perhaps wherever the first migrations of Africa relocated in the world, before modern religions like the Brahmin, the Hebraic, Christian, and Islamic instituted racist and patriarchal beliefs condoned by Brahman, YHWH Elohim, God, Allah. It is possible to assert that the principles of Maat exist in modern religions like precious jewels surrounded by justifications of lower thoughts. Some see the jewels. Perhaps ancient cultural memories return reified by knowledge—truth.

CHAPTER 3
The Afrocentric Theory of Education

The Afrocentric educational model is culturally oriented and ultimately adaptable to the needs of pupils and teachers. It lays a framework for building ideas that can assist in the cognitive and psychological development of children as an aid to critical thinking and cultural identity. You will find evidence of curricula and syllabi in the book *The Afrocentric School [a blueprint]* that you can build upon. This teachers' and learners' Afrocentric guide is designed to influence how the teacher can develop lesson plans using the Afrocentric Education Model. Although this model is culturally Afrocentric, it means that it is human-centric in that the use of this model ultimately seeks to move away from hierarchies of inferiority and superiority and domination to help us plan a more ethical way of being in the world especially for those who have newly come into the world. A severely problematic issue or concern for this one human origin model is that the dominant cultures that rule the world are essentially patriarchal, racist, and devoted by any means necessary to maintaining their dominance over minds, energies and the resources of the world. How many lives have been lost to arrive at this point in human history and development underscored by a past of ruin and underdevelopment for some? It will be difficult, therefore, and even impossible for some who read this work, who are grounded in racist patriarchal beliefs that underpin the current social hierarchies, including "education," to believe in respecting our African ancestors, the first people.

I must underscore that this model, while challenging white supremacy and the construction of race is not a Black nationalist model of education and will attempt to produce the knowledge that can show the significance of Afrocentric education to all humanity despite phenotypical differences. There is the recognition that certain phenotypes have collaborated to carry out the most heinous crimes to conquer the world for its precious resources whether mineral or human. At the same time, there have been phenotypes who have sought to find the most egalitarian ways to live. With the variations and mixtures of phenotypes, it is always the mind that can change whether from bad to good or good to bad. Culture is the method that can achieve becoming conscious, or unconscious based on the two major orientations that I have previously defined. However, from the Afrocentric vantage, there is the belief based on ancient African values and beliefs that humans can change, particularly when they are aware of truth, which is the foundation of "education."

The Afrocentric paradigm is a metatheory created by Molefi Kete Asante (1988),[1] to enable people, particularly those of the darkest hue, to center themselves in a true and remarkable cultural history. The idea of a true history of Africa will challenge the current misinformation about Africa. The discipline of Africology places the love of Africa and African humanity at the forefront of its academic research and studies toward developing the African episteme—knowledge. The African episteme is ancient; its development has been interrupted and plagiarized and its roots falsified. Africology is an academic discipline whose students work toward claiming, reclaiming, rebuilding, and building upon a very ancient episteme—knowledge—truth that influenced the creation of ancient civilizations. This is a critical history that all humanity should know and remember. At the same time, students of Africology work toward developing new ways to understand and live in the world based on more civilized ideas that existed before modern barbarism.

The love of Africa stands in contradiction to how other disciplines define Africa and her people. It interrogates and opposes the concerted attempt to construct a false cultural history of Africa, the birthplace and mother of humanity. The history of humanity has been distorted and shaped to fit racist propaganda for those who control resources and knowledge. Horrific crimes have been committed for thousands of years against Black humanity, without respite. Professor Asante (1988, p. 6) says that:

---

[1]According to Asante, a metatheory is a concept that includes a multiplicity of theories. It may be called a paradigm. Afrocentric metatheory helps to understand, investigate, and interpret more clearly every aspect of what it is to be African in this world.

Afrocentricity does not convert you by appealing to hatred or lust or greed or violence. As the highest, most conscious ideology, it makes its points, motivates its adherents, and captivates the cautious by the force of its truth. You are the ultimate test ... At the apex of your consciousness, it becomes your life because everything you do is it.

The Afrocentric model of education is grounded in the story of humanity offering a culturally oriented pedagogy sensitive to the needs of students in the development of their cultural identity.[2] This education guidebook is the teacher's guide and companion to *The Afrocentric School [a blue-print]*. An objective is to enable the teacher to create lesson plans based on the ideas of the Afrocentric guidebook. In this way, the pupils will understand their lessons in relation to their skills development, as defined by grounded research.

Most valuable to the students is the component of truth, which is essential to this model and ultimately leads to critical thinking skills. Truth is the foundation of logic. It is therefore important to explain the Afrocentric perspective as part of the cognitive and psychological process of understanding the relevance of this pedagogic model and how to use it as a platform to teach from.

I offer the teacher/educator (she, he, they), a practical, research-based model for excellence in pedagogy derived from the best of our African philosophies and traditions. In providing a cultural historical background, it is hoped that the educator, teacher, or learner will understand more clearly the logic of using an Afrocentric model of knowledge as opposed to continuing to use the Eurocentric model, which in its determined hierarchicalization of humanity through the belief in the falsehood of race and patriarchy prevents us from finding out who we truly are.

The Eurocentric model offers a false history of humanity as a foundation for critical thought and human development, which ultimately does not work for anyone. The Eurocentric axiom in the United States persuades its potential adherents and devotees to justify human inequalities as the fault of humans possessed with natural genetic flaws that cannot change.

---

[2]Cultural identity is a concept developed by Cheikh Anta Diop that is viewed as the overarching human identity from which cultural unity may arise.

In this way, we can absolve ourselves of any blame or relationship with other humans who do not seem to represent us. We are asked to have faith in the disciplines that we are being taught, that there is no connection between the ignorant and the wise, you are one or the other. These disconnections, alienations, dislocations among us appear real through the purposeful social hierarchies created that over generations appear to be the result of genetically determined certain types of people. As Africologists, we look at the roots.

The Afrocentric educationist who is both teacher and learner uses a set of moral standards that can apply to understanding:

- Placing Africa at the center of human history.
- All humans are related to one African mother[3] genetically and culturally.
- What culture is.
- How culture shapes our beliefs and values.
- Cultural beliefs and their impact on the role of education and educationists.
- That people are teachable.
- The importance of the teacher and learner to providing knowledge that will enhance the pupil's understanding of life and her/his/their potential.
- Skills development expectations from the data.
- How race is a cultural construction.
- The impact of racism on the so-called "races" in the United States and abroad.
- Cultural inclusion rather than racial inclusion underpins concepts embodied in this Afrocentric model.
- A purpose of this Afrocentric model is that educators and learners from all parts of the world, in recognition of one humanity, can locate their own histories in a more grounded and truthful manner.
- It is possible chronologically to trace the movements of African humanity and our sojourn to populate different parts of the world.
- Our Ancestors are African and Black.

---

[3]The mother of Africa is named Eve in the Bible and Hawa in the Koran. She is neither; she existed thousands of years earlier than these creation stories.

The academic world is essentially the brain, and the repository of knowledge and information of the ages codified and used to formulate ideas that academic theories, ideas, and disciplines transmitted to the students who enter the world of literacy and academia. Universities are repositories of culturally oriented knowledge. The role of academicians is to develop ideas grounded in the theories applied to each discipline and archived in the houses of knowledge—educational institutions of higher learning. In the United States, Eurocentric ways of thinking predominate.

That means that most of the theories that we used to teach the disciplines, like history, anthropology, psychology, sociology, archaeology, Egyptology, botany, biology, art, mathematics, sciences, medicine, government, and economies, are racist. They are racist because historically, Eurocentric universities and academic disciplines were mainly developed during First Nations' conquest and African colonization and enslavement. The genocidal behaviors of violent conquerors created wealth that was often the foundation and financial support of universities that naturally formed an allegiance to their donators.

These allegiances were abundant, providing context for academic ideas justifying atrocities against humans whom they viewed as animals, for instance, housing captured humans and producing *human zoos*, displaying people in places like Crystal Palace in London was a popular idea in Europe (Asante & Dove, 2021; Lindqvist, 1996).[4] Saartjie Baartman (1789–1815), a South African woman of Khoekhoe heritage, was just such a victim, put on display as a specimen when she was alive and her body parts were put on display in London and Paris after she passed away. An appeal was made for her body parts to be returned to South Africa; she came home during the time of President Nelson Mandela. Notions of superiority and inferiority were created and fabricated through the imagination of the colonizers. These activities in the construction of "others" translated into ideas of evolution and changes, relating to nature and

---

[4]Lindqvist's book delves into the horrendous racist deeds committed against Africa mythologized as academic truths. Asante and Dove examine the influence of cultural orientation regarding civilization or barbarism, defining such differences in relation to historical and environmental experiences thousands of years after migrations out of Africa led to new ideas that abandoned the earliest beliefs in African matriarchy.

survival in nature. Biology exemplified and displayed the idea of the "survival of the fittest"[5] often attributed to Charles Darwin who used this concept after Herbert Spencer (1820) who coined the term *survival of the fittest* as a concept he saw arising from the work of Charles Darwin's theory of *natural selection.* Spencer states "Doubtless many who have looked at Nature with philosophic eyes, have observed that death of the worst and multiplication of the best, must result in the maintenance of a constitution in harmony with surrounding circumstances. That the average vigor of any race would be diminished, did the diseased and feeble habitually survive and propagate: and that the destruction of such through failure to fulfil some of the conditions to life, leaves behind those which are able to fulfil the conditions of life, and thus keeps up the average fitness to the conditions of life; are almost self-evident truths" (p. 445).

It is this kind of thinking, *survival of the fittest*, that is embodied in the current political movement that is steadily removing culturally oriented notions of Maat, existing in current more socialistic beliefs that highlight the caring for the poor, the sick, the needy, the disadvantaged, and so on. It is of significance to note that the older European universities like Cambridge and Oxford received much of their knowledge from Africa through the ancient universities like the University of Sankore in Timbuktu that arose in ancient Ghana. European academic theories arose, in the main, from the justification of, and profits from, the enslavement of African people (François, 2019). Of importance is the reality that the ancient knowledge or episteme that undergirds these disciplines were sourced from Africa prior to conquest. That is why this Afrocentric guide will explain and include the influence of Kemet, ancient Egypt, on Euro-Southwest Asian philosophical thought and academia.

The mind is a necessary component in shaping culture, which influences how we think, live, and act in the world. This Afrocentric guide is ultimately to teach all people inclusive of children our connectedness to each other from the personal to the global, from the non-racist vantage point. To accomplish this goal, a central theme of this guide is to learn the

---

[5]Spencer (1864, vol. 1, p. 444) also stated: "This, which I have here sought to express in mechanical terms, is that which Mr. Darwin has called 'natural selection', or the preservation of favoured races in the struggle for life."

complexities and intersections between patriarchy, race, and racism that have divided and dislocated humanity.

The Afrocentric model recognizes that all teachers and learners come from complex and culturally oriented backgrounds and that these experiences influence how we view each other and our personal and social roles. Therefore, as potential educators, who we are and our experiences matter, they will have an impact on the children/pupils and our colleagues, friends, and families. The idea that humans will be unbiased is a figment of Eurocentric academic imagination ensconced in ethnographical research that feeds the academic disciplines with evidence that supports their existence. Simply put, when one believes in the inferiority or superiority of humans based upon the color and gender of a person or people, one is biased not only in thought but in action, in developing research and study. It is, however, possible to identify one's own bias and become less so. Another point is that the spiritual aspects of beingness are often discounted in our connectedness with each other particularly in European academia. However, our spirituality is just as powerful in a classroom or institution as in a church, mosque, temple, or other holy site. What is important for the reader to know is that Afrocentricity is not a religion and to become Afrocentric is not to become religious. Asante (2007, p. 22) says:

> Afrocentricity is an intellectual idea that suggests that African people must be viewed and must view themselves as agents in the historical process ... my political ideology is my own business. What does it matter that I am a Black Nationalist, Marxist, Democrat, Republican, Socialist or Anarchist? My religious faith is my business. What does it matter that I am an atheist, Christian, Jew, Yoruba, Muslim or Shintoist? Afrocentricity as a way of interpreting reality begins with the idea that it is teachable and accessible to anyone who cares to learn it ... the Afrocentrist will teach anyone how to become a scholar who begins the study of African people and African phenomena from the standpoint of Africans as subjects rather than objects of history.

The idea is to become more knowledgeable. Wisdom and knowledge of the past certainly play a key role in the cultural history of humanity and in creating a foundation for the discipline of Africology.

CHAPTER 4

Remembering Kemet and Ancient African Forebears

There are many societies that maintain African cultural beliefs and values have been made invisible when discussing race, as they are phenotypically different from Eurocentric stereotypical African phenotypes. Ancient African teachings and philosophies that brought civilization to the world provided the most democratic and balanced orientation that we are aware of. Importantly, they were mother-centered, in that the mother was revered and respected (Dove, 2002). The Afrocentric teacher recognizes the social and cultural system of mother-led societies as African matriarchy, which is based on the balance and harmony between the woman and the man as the foundation of these societies as it was with the civilization of Kemet. I see Kemet as central to the metatheory of Africology that represents the cultural values and beliefs that broadly existed across ancient Africa. However, the site of Kemet in Africa has been and is continually contested, in some cases violently. There have been many invasions and conquerors, but the latest are the Arabs who are claiming like the Europeans before them who created Egyptology that Kemet is not a Black civilization. The ancient Nubian and Kushite people quite possibly the original Kemites have been captured in their homelands of northeast and eastern Africa (including Egypt, Sudan, Ethiopia, Somalia, Kenya, Eritrea, Uganda, and eastern Congo). Even in the 21st century, they are being colonized by the Arabs through the religion of Islam and prevented from speaking their ancient language and practicing their ancient religious beliefs under threat of death. These ancient people founded Ta Seti, who, according to Prof Robin Walker (2006) of London, existed in 5,900 BCE, before Kemet was built, and it is believed that they were involved in the early development of Kemet.[1] Ancient artifacts, found by Professor Bruce Williams in the Qustul site, showed that the Kushites and Nubians had Per aa (Pharaonic) dynasties.

The discipline of Egyptology, grounded in race theory, attempts to claim overall that the African origin of Kemet was European. The Northern part of Africa is viewed as an important point of entry for the development of civilization by Europeans coming across the Mediterranean. This was disproved by Cheikh Anta Diop and Theophile Obenga, his student, at the Cairo Symposium on the peopling of ancient Egypt and the deciphering of Meroitic script held January 28 to February 3, 1974 (Diop et al., 1997). They proved that chronologically, Black/Africans came down the Nile River from the center of Africa and populated North Africa thousands of years earlier than the Mediterranean civilizations who were generally Africans of a lighter shade whose cultural affiliation was with Northern cradle beliefs were evident in the practices of the Greeks who owned enslaved people and disrespected women.

Since we are all African, it is important to understand how culture differentiates us. In his historical contextualization of the birth of the Negro myth, Cheikh Anta Diop (1991a, p. 1) refers to Herodotus, a Greek historian who visited Kemet and whose works as an observer are used often by modern historians to understand the social conditions of the time. By current historians, he is considered mad if he speaks respectfully of Black Africans and considered sane and valuable regarding his general observations when color is not included.

When Herodotus visited Egypt, it had already lost its independence a century earlier. Conquered by the Persians (Iranians) in 525 BCE, from then on it was continually dominated by the foreigner: after the Persians came the Macedonians under Alexander (333 BC), the Romans under Julius Caesar (50 BC), the Arabs in the 7th century, the Turks in the 16th century, the French with Napoleon, then the English at the end of the 19th century. Ruined by all these successive invasions, Egypt, or perhaps

---

[1]Professor Walker uses the dating of the priest Manetho to correct the problematic of Egyptologists who led by Eduard Meyer use the Berlin Timeline to reduce the chronology to fit into a time when it might be possible for Europeans to be civilized according to definitions of civilization.

more aptly put, the Nile Valley, the cradle of civilization for 10,000 years while the patriarchal racist and non-indigenous world was steeped in barbarism would no longer play a political role. Nevertheless, it would long continue to initiate the younger Mediterranean peoples (Greeks and Romans) among others into the enlightenment of civilization. Throughout antiquity, it would remain the classic land where the Mediterranean peoples went on pilgrimages to drink at the fount of scientific, religious, moral, and social knowledge, the most ancient of such knowledge that mankind had acquired that we know of.

The latest invaders, the Arabic Islamic rulers, claimed that Kemet was Arabic, they compete with Europeans in the claim for ownership, but now under Islamic jurisdiction, they control the artifacts and evidence of its Black African origin. This claim helps with Islamic ideas of civilization and tourism. From this vantage point, the theories of race and evolution that inferiorized the African make Kemet's African origin appear to be an impossibility. However, the chronology of human existence makes these false claims unfeasible, illogical, and ludicrous. Some Egyptologists or students of Kemet like Count de Volney, Gerald Massey, Cheikh Anta Diop, George James, William Leo Hansberry, Drusilla Dunjee Houston, Anthony Browder, Kimani Nehusi, Solanje Ashby, Deidre Wimby, Virgina Spottswood Simon, Sally-Ann Ashton, Katiuscia Rubeiro, Ma'at Ka Re Monges, Molefi Kete Asante, and many others apply truth and logic to ground their assertions. Cheikh Anta Diop followed the chronology of humanity to prove his assertions, which he first wrote in his book *The African Origin on Civilization*, published in 1967 in France and then translated to English in 1974.

After visiting Egypt in 1783, Count de Volney (1991[1791]) wrote *Ruins of Empires*. His work was essentially heretical in content when referring to his findings guided by the Genius:

> Those piles of ruins, said he, which you see in that narrow valley watered by the Nile are the remains of opulent cities, the pride of the ancient kingdom of Ethiopia ... There a people, now forgotten, discovered, while others were yet barbarians, the elements of the arts and sciences. A race of men now rejected from society for their *sable skin and frizzled hair*, founded on the study of the laws of nature, those civil and religious systems

which still govern the universe … whereby means beyond vulgar reach, a genius, profound and bold, established institutions which have weighed on the whole human race. (pp. 13–19)

For the discipline of Africology, this ancient knowledge is essential. Africans, whose ancestors were stolen from Africa, have a special case to seek cultural relocation: Who am I? Where am I? How did I get here? The invention of African history and African inferiority is intrinsic to race theory, which of necessity omits the history of humanity, of which we all are a part of, and have a right to know. The laws of Maat are the oldest codified set of virtues and morals that guide humans to become virtuous. These laws are ensconced in modern religions. Ultimately, the laws of Maat reveal that one is judged not based on how one looks, melanin content of the skin, height, number of limbs, whether one has sight or hearing, genders, sexuality, physical and mental abilities, finances, etc., but on how one lives to make the world a better place for humanity (Asante & Dove, 2021). Such standards apply to how one becomes an ancestor (Ephirim-Donkor, 1997).

The Weighing of the Heart is symbolic of one's heart being weighed against Maat's feather of truth that will indicate whether one has lived a life deserving of ancestor hood in the spiritual realm. The feather of truth sits on one side of scales of justice with the heart of the deceased on the other side. Djehuti, the keeper of wisdom, can appear at the top center of the scale of justice represented in the image of a baboon known for intelligence. Also, Maat can appear in the top center of the scales. In the case of the high priests Ani and Tutu who are married, it is Djehuti on the top of the scales that is also represented as a baboon. Djehuti is also the Ibis-headed divinity. In this guise, he takes note of the lives lived by the departed. If the hearts of Ani and Tutu weigh more than Maat's feather of truth, their hearts would be devoured by Ammit the devourer, who stands behind Djehuti, and such a person could not become an ancestor. If the hearts of Ani and Tutu were lighter than Maat's feather of truth, it was believed that they would be embraced by the divinity Asar whose wife Aset and her sister Neb-het stand together by his throne. Ani and Tutu will undergo other tests, described further in the text, of ultimately becoming divine ancestors. One can only become an ancestor if one tries to live in Truth, Justice, Righteousness, Reciprocity, Harmony, Balance, and Order.

While this is an ancient African belief from Kemet (Nehusi, 2016). If one's heart is heavier than the feather of truth, the divine Ammit who is part crocodile, hippopotamus, and leopard will consume the corrupted heart, thereby ridding the world of evil. She is divine and never corrupted or tainted by her divine service to humanity and the cosmos. Trying to live a good life to become an ancestor is still practiced among many African people today, despite cultural impositions (Ephirim-Donkor, 2021).

Moreover, to recognize and revere an ancestor is an important part of a spiritual connection culturally. Maat provides the standards by which we may still measure good behavior. The irony is that Maatic principles are embedded in modern religions that despise the humanity of the Black/African people. It can be said that the culture of a person influences how one interprets meaning. It is entirely possible that the laws of Maat can become a superficial and unachievable belief in a society that is patriarchal and racist. We may find that this is the case in teaching this model. However, we are all learning and growing. The love of knowledge and wisdom is fundamental in this education model. The educator/teacher is the living example of becoming that is being promoted to the pupil who is in turn becoming. Learning is the path for wisdom. It is not correct for us to teach what we do not believe in, and that is why it is incumbent on teachers and learners to understand the book *The Afrocentric School [a blueprint]*, which is for all children. Below is the *Weighing of the Heart* of Hunefer, painted by the author. You can find the *Weighing of the Heart* of Ani and Tutu painted by me on the cover of *The Afrocentric School [a blueprint]*.

CHAPTER 5

Culture and Knowledge (Institutionalized)

The Ethiopian Queen Makeda (1005–955 BCE) ruled the kingdom of Saba or Sheba in Ethiopia and Yemen, controlling the trading of the Red Sea (Walker, 2006, pp. 85–87). Her father was Shar Habil, a king from Yemen, and her mother Ekeye Azeb, a princess from Ethiopia. The wise and talented ruler visited King Solomon of Israel with whom she bore a son, Menelik, who began a line of an Ethiopian and Israeli political and religious amalgamation. She said of wisdom:

> I am smitten with the love of wisdom, and I am constrained by the cords of understanding; for wisdom is far better than a treasure of gold and silver. It is sweeter than honey, and it maketh one to rejoice more than wine, and it illumineth more than the sun, and it is to be loved more than precious stones … Wisdom is an exalted thing and a rich thing; I will love her like a mother, and she will embrace me like her child. (Busby, 1992, p. 16)

An Afrocentric teacher and learner must understand that most Eurocentric history has been constructed to silence the voices of those impacted by colonization and enslavement. The Afrocentric orientation values the voice of those silenced throughout centuries of violent encroachment on less aggressive and more egalitarian societies whose lives and lands were taken aggressively. The proposed amalgamation between the Black Hebrews and the White Hebrews rose in the public eye during the famine in Ethiopia when the African Black Falasha Hebrews were suffering with everyone else during the 1980s.

The highly publicized air transportation in 1985 when Shimon Peres, the prime minister of Israel, welcomed this entry as a humane act in the belief that there were no "Black and White Jews only Jews" (Kessler, 1996,

p. xi). Today, these same Black African Hebrews are at the bottom of the society that saved their lives. They were saved to inherit sacred knowledge from the ancient history of the Falasha, such knowledge is worth more than gold. Today, these ancient Hebrews are debased under the auspices of white supremacy firmly ensconced in modern Israel where Black African Jews languish at the bottom of all the social hierarchies as *Blacks*. It has been said that the Black/African Hebrews were not allowed into the Israeli bomb shelters during the 2025 bombings from Iran on June 16 in retaliation for the bombing of Iran on June 13, 2025. The Iranians are known in ancient history as the Persians who conquered Kemet in 525 to 404 BCE under the reign of Cambyses II, called by the Kemetic name, Mesuti Ra. During this time, Greek students like Pythagoras and Plato came to study at the universities in Kemet. Note that the Queen or Kandake Makeda's father was a King or Per aa from Yemen and trading along the Red Sea. The Yemen history and relationship with Ethiopia and Israel and its great antiquity have been erased. The conquests by Islam and the British have created havoc, cultural imposition has dominated through its colonization and battles. Regarding cultural identity, the Yemenis who are also ancient people are physically Yemenis, but mentally they are pursuing the religious and political beliefs that have been imposed upon them, it is possible to say that their ancient spiritual practices pre Hebrew, Christianity, Islam were more closely aligned with Kemet.

Although the teacher must seek to dismantle race theory through knowledge, it is wise to remember that racism still exists in the actions and minds of perpetrators and victims. The call for dismantling and transforming the race discourse is futuristic and is similar to the day that enslavement was abolished in the United States. Nothing changed, but it began a process. Minds and action had to function to accept a vision of possibilities within a cultural orientation that focused on profit. It was the cultural orientation that focused on Maatic principles that came through in the zone of confluence where these competing cultures met.

The Afrocentric model does not deny the impact of the belief in race— white supremacy, as a genetic-based theory, taught for over 500 years, and accepts that it will be difficult to accommodate new ideas as plans of our futures have been based on this falsehood, inculcated deeply in our minds and behaviors. The Afrocentric model is futuristic in making provision for a new pedagogy and way of thinking that will take time to understand and enact but must be done. One cannot hold back the tide.

The theory of race arose from the justification of patriarchy and domination. There is no more justification for patriarchy than for race. Both are cultural constructions in which neither the woman, whatever her sexuality, class, or phenotype, nor melaninated people of whatever sex, gender, sexuality, class, or phenotypes deserve abuse and possibly death, certainly more likely the darker one is. In terms of patriarchy, race, gender, and sexuality, when evaluating the status of the woman or those closer to identifying as women; women have a lower human value than men generally in patriarchy, and in the race paradigm, the darker she is the less valued. As already noted, the belief in race gives the white woman a special position; thus, although below the white man in the social hierarchy, she is above all the other men and women. In contrast, the darkest African woman, because of her gender and color, is placed below all other women and men. The identical and more ancient anti-Black woman's belief is located in the modern religions of Brahminism, Abrahamism, Christianity, and Islam through holy creation and other stories made to suit the cultural orientation of the devotees.

The justification for the conquering, colonizing, and enslaving of African people in Africa and across the world is still upheld with pride and satisfaction within academic disciplines in European universities. This pride is taught openly, or covertly through the theory of evolution where the European and Arab are considered culturally and socially advanced through a contrived history of humanity. The theory of evolution is grounded in a belief in African inferiority and European superiority. White supremacy is foundational to all the major academic disciplines parading as universal natural law; it is a dogma encompassed in European cultural thought and belief, revealing its presence in philosophy, behavior, education, religion, governance to entertainment and politics, etc. In contrast to Count de Volney's recognition of Kemet and the contribution of Africa to world development, Georg Wilhelm Friedrich Hegel (1770–1831), one of Europe's most important and highly esteemed philosophers, wrote of Africa:

It has no historical interest of its own, for we find its inhabitants living in barbarism and savagery in a land which has not furnished them with any integral ingredient of culture. From its earliest historical times, Africa has remained cut off from all contacts with the rest of the world; it is the land of gold, forever pressing in upon itself, and the land of childhood, removed from the light of self-conscious history and wrapped in the dark mantle of night ... man as we find him in Africa has not progressed beyond his immediate existence. As soon as man emerges as a human being, he stands in opposition to nature, and it is this along which makes him a human being. But if he has merely made a distinction between himself and nature, he is still at the first stage of his development: he is dominated by passion and is nothing more than a savage ... The negro is an example of animal man in all his savagery and lawlessness, and if we are to understand him at all, we must put aside all our European attitudes. (Hegel, 1975, p. 174)

These Eurocentric philosophical ideas, heralded and respected by the world, have been critical to justifying the debasement and enslavement of African people, once the scientists and educators of humanity. The lands of the indigenous people yielded immense wealth and power to build academic institutions. Powerful universities like Harvard, Columbia, Princeton, Yale, and Cambridge in the UK have admitted to benefiting from profits made from the enslavement of African people from the continent although clearly they benefited from building on the lands of the original people and erasing the African academic roots of their knowledge (Smith & Ellis, 2017).

Early benefactors who gave money to Brown and Harvard, for instance, made their fortunes running "*slave*" ships to Africa and milling cotton from plantations in the American South. Georgetown could afford to offer free tuition to its earliest students by virtue of the unpaid labor of Jesuit-owned slaves on plantations in Maryland. At the University of Virginia, founded and designed by Thomas Jefferson, *slaves* cooked and cleaned for the sons of the Southern Gentry.

Universities like Cambridge were advantaged by enslavement and claimed that the whole of the United Kingdom profited institutionally, from banking to museums, parks, properties, royal mail, and so on (François, 2019).

As argued by Dove (1993), of significance and often omitted from the concept of "colonial education" was the imposition of elite European schools across Africa that reflected the elite public schools in Britain.

They promoted the logic of the superiority of colonial leadership, colonial administrators and the training of doctors, chemists, civil servants, academics of every discipline, as well as scientists (Leinster-Mackay, 1988, p. 8). The taxes enforced (sometimes violently) on African people were used to support these "public" (elite) schools across Africa, not unlike the taxes in the southern United States, populated predominantly by Africans after enslavement, when state schools initiated by Africans relied on their taxes to provide the monies to facilitate the "education" of European (white) children.

Dove (1993) further linked, the imperialist public schooling to Free Masonry as a critical component in the colonial power structure and a central part of the "old boy" network (Rich, 1988). In this way, Free Masonry produced high-ranking imperialists ranging from secret service agents, government officials to members of the royal family. From an Afrocentric perspective using chronology, one understands that these Eurocentric Free Masons were disconnected from the history of Free Masonry, which is rooted in ancient Africa, and Kemet is an early reference to it. No one knows how to build the pyramids today or cut the stones so precisely and lay them in the necessary formation that would last thousands of years and be a mathematical, geometric, astrological, astronomical, scientific miracle of masonry.

This historical reality regarding the theoretical basis for knowledge production in university repositories is reflected in school curricula. Thus, Africans, Indians, Europeans, Chinese, Japanese, Malaysian people, etc., living and studying in the United States can be unaware of how racism is embedded in academic disciplines from the beginning to the end of life. Without knowledge of historical truths, people are more likely to believe in the "melting pot" democratic diversity idea of the United States and, in this way, believe that we naturally fall into our rightful social positions. Foreign and national policies continue to reflect these beliefs and actions through culturally formed institutional structures culturally insensitive to "other" non-whites. Diop's (1991a, pp. 132–134) research on nation state constructions describes models of the nation state that manifest the conditions of genocide like the United States. The nation state that most closely resembles the United States is known as the Spartan type. Sparta was a Greek nation state arising in 900 BCE that prioritized its military power.

> If for whatever reason, the conquering group refuses to mix with the indigenous conquered element and bases its domination on this absolute separation, the opposition is essentially ethnic and will always be resolved, in ancient and modern history, by genocide ... the three Americas, including Canada, in varying degrees, Australia, New Zealand, Tasmania, Scandinavia up to a point; Greenland, South Africa, a large part of Asia ... most of the present states of the modern world belong to the model of the state founded on genocide; it is not the exception, rather the general rule, which encompasses three quarters of all dry land. (Diop, 1991a, pp. 132–133)

The ancient Spartan model helps to explain the nature of the nation state and the institutions that support it (Dove, 2002). The institution of education should be understood as culturally oriented to suit the needs of the nation state. Thus, universities, schools, nurseries, etc. maintain a belief in the state, which is often responsible for their funding. It should be of interest that the genocide of the First Nations people has been paramount in helping to create all the nations in the Americas—North, South, and Central.

The intention of Afrocentric theory is to identify and fight all oppressions. Molefi Kete Asante (2003) who has studied the specific survival struggles of Black people in the Americas for over 60 years defines Afrocentricity as:

> [A] mode of thought and action in which the centrality of African interests, values and perspectives predominate. In regard to theory, it is the placing of African people in the center of any analysis of African phenomena. Thus, it is possible for anyone to master the discipline of seeking the location of Africans in a given phenomenon. In terms of action and behavior, it is a devotion to the idea that what is in the best interests of African consciousness is at the heart of ethical behavior. Finally, Afrocentricity seeks to enshrine the idea that blackness itself is a trope of ethics. Thus, to be Black is to be against all forms of oppression, homophobia, patriarchy, child abuse, pedophilia, and white racial domination. (p. 2)

This model seeks to help us to become conscious of the accomplishments and joys as well as the ills of humanity. Maat provides an Africological guide to make assertions about what is human and inhuman. It is only possible to correct inhumane behaviors if we know how to identify them. In this guidebook, culture, not race, is perceived to be the biggest difference among humans in the way that we think and behave. It is possible, then, for us to change. Through Afrocentricity, we assert that the battle is for the mind. The concept of culture will be defined and examined. The mind is as intrinsic to the development of culture as culture is to the development of the mind.

CHAPTER 6
Cheikh Anta Diop's Two-Cradle Theory

All cultural groups have an interest in investing in the development of their people so that members may survive and flourish individually and collectively. Within this cultural matrix, the love of one's humanity is a vital component. If the culture that you live in despises your humanity, it is not your culture. Clearly, in varying societal structures across the world, this has been the case for Black African people even ruling their own colonized countries on the continent. Not only African people have found the reality that the culture they live in, develop, and give their lives to (e.g., fighting foreign wars, demanding social change, challenging injustices) despises their humanity. This hatred for the Black person was given as a reason that Muhammad Ali, at one time the world's finest boxer, chose to go to prison for 7 years ("Muhammad Ali refuses to fight in Vietnam" (1967, n.d.):

> Why should they ask me to put on a uniform and go 10,000 miles from home and drop bombs and bullets on Brown people in Vietnam while so-called Negro people in Louisville are treated like dogs and denied simple human rights? No, I'm not going 10,000 miles from home to help murder and burn another poor nation simply to continue the domination of white slave masters of the darker people the world over. This is the day when such evils must come to an end. I have been warned that to take such a stand would cost me millions of dollars. But I have said it once and I will say it again. The real enemy of my people is here. I will not disgrace my religion, my people or myself by becoming a tool to enslave those who are fighting for their own justice, freedom and equality.

Vital to the shaping of a society is the molding of the mind and the intellect; how they evolve is crucial to the development of cultural identity and thus the knowledge of self and society. For those whose ancestors were conquered, enslaved, and colonized, the development of African cultural identity has been compromised, altered, and corrupted through the lens of race—white supremacy and the systematic efforts that have endured for centuries, to culturally impose ideas as well as actions that debase, demoralize, and demonize Africa and her people, as if they are true. The identity that is being culturally imposed is racial identity, a lie.

Cheikh Anta Diop (1996), conscious of the falsification of African history, taught that developing cultural identity was critical to the formation of cultural unity. The idea is that cultural identity is the overarching identity that connects people to their cultural beliefs and values. He found that to be the case in Africa. Cultural identity enables people to view their status within their cultures in their other roles or identities. An African, First Nations, Chinese, Indonesian, or Japanese mother may be viewed as a respected person in one culture and disrespected in another and yet she is still a mother, and she will be treated accordingly. Diop's life's research as a continental Black African anthropologist, sociologist, historian, linguist, Egyptologist, and nuclear scientist led him to understand that a cultural unity existed Africa-wide, in that there existed a commonality among African people relating to values, beliefs, and behaviors (e.g., respect for elders, ancestors, children, mothers, families, collective ideals). The fundamental similitude was based on the reciprocal relationship between the woman and the man, the creators of life and culture.

In the cradle theory, Diop proposes four major pillars of culture crucial to forming cultural identity: history, language, psychology, and spirituality. In other words, one can choose to develop a cultural identity that enables the knowing of self, then it becomes possible to identify with others, regardless of imposed hierarchal differences, and recognize that cultural unity is possible. This idea is fundamental to the Authentic Model of Education being proposed. Below is a simple understanding of the pillars of cultural identity (Dove, 2015, pp. 110–112).

1. *The History of People is:*

The cultural "glue" that unifies a community with a sense of belonging is that its collective experiences over time are part of a historical continuity. It provides a consciousness that enables people to identify themselves as part of a population connected in ways that define their traditional similarities and distinctions from other cultural groups. People want to understand, appreciate, and live their historical legacy and transmit their knowledge, cultural memory, or heritage to their descendants.

2.   *The Language of People is:*

Founded on the sound and tone of communication that people emit to transmit cultural beliefs and values in relation to expounding on their explanations. It is foundational to people's understanding of each other. Language enables the exchange of and passing on of knowledge to specifically enhance existence and connectivity. It also transmits ideals, hopes, aspirations, directives, thoughts, conveying spoken and musical expressions that can evoke all manner of emotional states, movements, and healing. The utterance of speech is known as Nommo by the Dogon people of Mali, and the sound and vibration of it impact the environment either making harmonious or not, Maatic—ordered or Isfetic—chaotic. In other words, utterances have power.

3.   *The Psychology of People is:*

Based on the study of the human mind and derived from the Greek word psyche, itself rooted in the KMT word sakhu,[1] essentially the "soul of being." The psyche underpins the development of identity, personality, and consciousness. The study of the human mind and human behavior cannot be separated from an exploration of matters of the spirit as they shape concepts of humanity and understandings of "self" and provide a clear sense of one's spiritual connection to the universe. It contributes to personal and societal development and potential futures that connect to the heart and sense of feeling.

4.   *Spirituality of People is:*

Based on a belief that there exists a Higher Order of power that humans are connected to which can be accessed using certain rituals. People feel the power and connections with each other. This power is used to support, justify, and fulfill the needs of the cultural collective. Spiritual systems provide

---

[1]The concept of seeking the Sakhu is from the work of African psychologist Wade Nobles (2006).

access to power differently and are shaped and influenced by cultural beliefs, values, and rituals. These rituals may be inclusive of music, dance, prayers, shaking, speaking in tongues, etc. Names are given to identify the spiritual sources of power (e.g., Creator, Amun, Yahweh, God, Allah, Brahma, Olodumare, Nyame) and so on.

In this Afrocentric Education Model, the four pillars of history, language, psychology, and spirituality are viewed as important cultural prerequisites for developing cultural identity among the educators/teachers and pupils. The reality is that we have common ancestors who shaped the world. The potential for this educational enterprise is that we become located or relocated in the story of humanity and eventually understand when and why our paths as human beings changed, and how and why we humans separated and formed the cultures that distinguish us in ways that very often evoke perpetual wars. The pursuance of this knowledge can enable us to develop the potential to reconnect and form a cultural unity, not just as continental Black Africans as proposed by Diop but as human beings across the world recognizing and celebrating differences as a basis of peace and harmony with each other, the environment and the cosmos bereft of hierarchies and fear.

THE NEED FOR CULTURAL IDENTITY

History

People without history are people without knowledge of who they were, where they are, and who they may become.

> The events which transpired 5,000 years ago; five years ago, or five minutes ago, have determined what will happen five minutes from now; five years from now or 5,000 years from now. All history is a current event. (John Henrik Clarke, quoted in Browder, 1992, p. 5)

The Arabic and European conquests of Africa and the enslavement of her people required the disruption, debasement, and devaluation of African cultural history. Cultural identity became disordered. The Euro-Southwest Asians fabricated a history in which African women and men had no history of worth, and were immoral and even subhuman. The philosopher

Georg Wilhelm Friedrich Hegel (1975), who never went to Africa, and is still considered one of Europe's greatest philosophers, said of Africa:

> It has no historical interest of its own, for we find its inhabitants living in barbarism and savagery in a land which has not furnished them with any integral ingredient of culture. From the earliest historical times, Africa has remained cut off from all contacts with the rest of the world; it is the land of gold, forever pressing in upon itself, and the land of childhood, removed from the light of self-conscious history and wrapped in the dark mantle of night. Its isolation is not just a result of its tropical nature, but an essential consequence of its geographical character. (p. 174)

Hegel was not alone in his conception and construction of African history; he fully comprehended and benefited from the enslaving of African people. The enlightenment period for European philosophers like Renee Descartes, John Locke, Thomas Hobbes, Jean-Jacques Rousseau from the 16th century had imagined human origins as foundational to their philosophical thoughts and early definitions of the hierarchies as human races were being developed (Asante & Dove, 2021). William Petty had written by 1676, *Of the Scale of Creatures*, advancing his belief in the mental superiority, behavior, and color of Europeans whom he believed were a separate species to Africans (Lewis, 2012). Other pseudo-scientists were soon to follow.

For a clear description of the pseudo-sciences involved in the belief in and construction of race, please read Stephen J. Gould's (1981) book *The Mismeasure of Man*. The book *Being Human Being* by Molefi Kete Asante and Nah Dove (2021) lays out the context of how these cultural beliefs arose and some of the ways that they have impacted on humanity.

The falsehood of race has been challenged by the identification of the many civilizations that arose from Africa, including KMT (ancient Egypt), the earliest known nation state, although it is said that Ta Seti, Kush/Nubia, considered a Queendom or Kingdom arose earlier. Both Ta Seti and Kemet are considered culturally African, aided in part by cultural values, beliefs, artifacts, sciences, and linguistic and spiritual similitude across the African continent. Later, when the Kings and Queens of Kush/Nubia returned to Kemet in the 25th dynasty, even the Egyptologists who have falsely claimed Kemet as a European civilization, admitted to the fact that the Kushites who returned to Kemet in the 25th dynasty as the ruling Per aas, bringing back African matriarchal beliefs, was Black African. Diop, who was a nuclear physicist, applied his melanin content tests on finding out the level of the melanin content of the mummified remains of the Per aa. Although not allowed to test the melanin content of the older mummified rulers of Kemet, Diop was able to apply his melanin count analysis on mummies of later dynastic rulers such as Ramesses III. He reported on the melanin count at the Cairo Symposium in 1974 (Diop et al., 1997). "Diop found that the melanin in the skin of four 19th century BCE Per aa mummies was comparable to the concentration in his own skin … However, his findings provoked a reaction … he was never allowed to obtain any more mummy skin again" (Finch III, 2023, p. 23). Below is a painting from the tomb of the Per aa Rameses III who in 1230 became Per aa in Kemet. Later Rameses launched voyages across the Atlantic to Ancient America (Walker, 2006, p. 675).

The paintings of the phenotypes below who lived in and also conquered Kemet are from the tomb of Per aa Ramses III.

A is the Kemite. B is the Indo-European; C represents the Kushite/Nubian, and D the Semite.

A.   B.   C.   D.

The first waves of foreign conquests recorded in Africa date back to Kemet (ancient Egypt), they included the Hyksos, Assyrians, Persians, Greeks, Romans, Arabs, and Turks. These conquests heralded the dawn of invasion across the continent. Arabian and European enslavers and colonialists continued going further South, bringing their religions with them. Ancient West African societies, such as Ancient Ghana (Mali and Mauritania) and Tekrur (Senegal) were also forced to contend with colonists and enslavers until the present. These cultural impositions changed the histories of indigenous Africans as languages and ancestral lines of communication were prevented. Ironically, African knowledge, ranging from the spiritual and scientific to the literal and creative, along with people's attributes, lands, and resources, contributed to the expansion of these conquering societies and the economic development of their nation states in their home countries.

Language

During conquests, cultural imperialism took place, which included the removal of language and the changing of the names of historical places. Language is the way that people communicate who they are and make sense of everything that is dear to them. They transmit their values, beliefs, practices, ways of venerating their ancestors, traditions, and even how to fight for their liberty. In the case of Africa and African people, Europeans and Arabian conquerors established their languages as the major languages. Currently, in the Sudan, the Kushite/Nubian people of Ta Seti, are still being enslaved, forced from their lands, and forbidden to speak their own languages. Arabic language does not respect African/Black humanity: *abd* is the name used to define the African/Black person as a slave (Jok, 2001). *Abd* is used interchangeably to describe an obscene person lacking moral stature, a filthy person, a person practicing a non-Muslim religion, or the Nuba of South Sudan, who are enslaved by Arabians. New names were created, giving new meanings to the lands, resources, and people they control. The whole of Africa has been invaded, and the people's dominant languages for each of the newly created nation states are European and/or Arabic. The majority of African Americans brought to North America as enslaved Africans were able to create linguistic systems. According to anthropologist Melville Herskovits (1990) African people created intonations and words recognizable across languages. It was believed that European and African languages had no similarities. However, enslaved African people found that some African words and English words were almost identical in meaning and sound. European enslavers thought that African people did not pronounce words correctly. They just preferred their own speech. Ebonics is evidence of that. African humanity was the first, and thus, logically all languages are traceable to Africa, as is writing which has been proven (Shevoroshkin, 1990).

Psychology

Over the centuries, the psyche and psychology of African people have been undermined because of the belief in the inferiority of Black people of every gender within the economic, political, spiritual, and social hierarchies. Race and racism have had psychological ramifications for all people but particularly regarding the safety and survival of African people. Black psychologists and psychiatrists like Frantz Fanon, Asa Hilliard, Joy DeGruy, Frantz Fanon, Bobby Wright, Frances Cress Welsing, Na'im Akbar, Wade Nobles, Amos Wilson, and J. Owusu-Bempah developed the Eurocentric discipline of psychology to include the psychological impact of racist experiences of African/Black people as well as defining the nature of white supremacy. Wade Nobles rooted the discipline back to Kemet with the inclusion of the spiritual aspect of psychology and Howitt and Owusu-Bempah (1994) rooted the discipline in its racist foundations in philosophy and theory while identifying its racist role in defining the "inferior" *mind* of Black people which in this work is understood as critical to the shaping of the culture as the culture is to the shaping of the mind:

> [P]sychology continues to treat racism largely as something apart from itself, something the discipline studies, and not what it does. How can psychology seem so unconcerned about racism and at the same time claim to serve humanity? ... In this regard, the discipline seems best characterized as a cultural artifact, to be understood more or less as any institution in a racist society. Like all professionals, it exemplifies a struggle amongst, and for, the vested interests of its members. But, more importantly, it frequently codifies and articulates the concerns and ideologies of dominant groups in society. (p. 8)

The psychology of oppression developed a new line of African thought called Black psychology, which is still not taught in the Pan European Academy. Africology embraces these important studies, which are records of thoughts regarding the psychology of the African mind under domination. As explained, the psyche cannot be separated from the mind.

Spirituality and Religion

In defining education or knowledge as the foundation for building cultural identity, it is important to show that cultural identity has been interrupted, debased, and replaced by racial identity. For Black/African people, the process of defamation has been a long-protracted journey of possibly 3,000 years when linked to Brahminism. The process of defamation was one of war and destruction. Every feature of life and culture had to be changed to fulfill the needs of conquerors. Truth had to be hidden and made insignificant so that lie could appear more palatable. A major part of cultural imposition and institutional transformation was/is through religion. This medium, embracing ideas of divinity and connection to the creator, was used effectively to impact mind, body, and spirit.

Foreign religions have impacted the spiritual systems of Africa from Kemet until now.[2] Brahmin, Abrahamic, Christian, and Islamic religions constructed a moral story in which the Blackest skinned woman and man lost their moral integrity. In the Hebraic, Christian, and Islamic creation stories, the mother of humanity (whom we know is African) is Eve, or Hawa, and the mother divinity of Kali is portrayed as Black with skulls hanging on a necklace around her neck, holding severed heads. In the Hebraic, Christian, Islamic, Eve or Hawa's supposed relationship with Satan questioned her morality, the authority of her husband, and wisdom of the male divinities God/Allah/Yahweh. In the case of the Black man, in the 6th century Babylonian Talmud of the Hebrew religion, the Black son of Noah of the ark, Ham, castrated his father (Asante & Dove, 2021). This baseless crime was contrived as the sin that condemned Ham's son Kush and his Black descendants, to be enslaved eternally to the descendants

---

[2]For a comprehensive understanding of patriarchy and enslavement in the religious demonization of the Black African mother and father, please read Asante and Dove (2021, pp. 53–88).

of Noah's other two sons, Japheth the white son and Shem the Semite or mixed "race" son. The later European pseudo-scientific constructions of race from the 1600s, are founded on these beliefs.

Brahmins or Hindus, much like Christians, Hebrews and Muslims, consider the Black person to be morally inferior as they do the woman as a mother. Like race, the *Rig Veda*, the holy text of the Brahmin religion, written in Sanskrit, defines four castes and five statuses. The castes are identified by the colors white, red, yellow, and black. White was associated with the (Aryan) Brahmins, the teachers, and priests; red with the Kshatriyas, the warriors; yellow with the Vaisyas, the merchants and farmers, while Black was associated with the Sudras, the lowest caste born as sinners, identifiable by their skin color, with no right to listen to the "holy" words or become literate to read them. The Sudra are slaves of the religion. They are the descendants of the original African people, the Harrapan, who were conquered. They were matriarchal, literate, and higher learners who built cities, the remains of which still exist today. Castes cannot mix. The Dalit, known as untouchables, is the forbidden progeny of mixed castes. They represent a caste excluded from the religion. They live as perpetual sinners and are considered outcastes who can never change their low status. They are perceived to be so beneath the other castes that their images cannot be held by the gaze of those more superior. The Lord Manu, who created humanity and made laws, says of women and Black men:

- To kill women and Sudras (Black humanity in the caste) one need not worry, for it is not a sin.
- He who weds a Sudra woman becomes an outcaste.
- A Brahmana who takes a Sudra woman to bed will sink into hell.
- If a Sudra mentions the names of the caste of the Brahmans or Kshatriyas, an iron nail ten fingers long shall be thrust hot into his mouth.
- If a Sudra hears the Vedas (the religious and holy texts), his ears shall be filled with molten lead. If he speaks with them, his tongue will be cut out; and if he memorizes them, his body cut to pieces. (Chandler, 1999, p. 133)

These religions and pseudo-sciences have played a critical role in maligning the character of Black humanity, particularly those of the darkest hue, justifying conquest, colonization, enslavement, and continuing mistreatment of Africa and Black people across the world.

The pillars of cultural identity are compromised by these conditions. Without knowledge to challenge these false assertions, assumptions, beliefs, ensconced in social institutions, there is little or no vision of how the so-called education could be, or how it has been. Educators, like everybody else, find themselves with no way to redress any bias or illogicity that they might perceive or sense. The complications of false historical and cultural information have corrupted cultural identities and divided humanity.

The Afrocentric Model serves to highlight culture and the accomplishments of African people (she, he, they), from ancient times until now. Countless educators have contributed to the development of Afrocentric theory, which could not exist without thousands of years of foundational and historical knowledge, much of which has been plagiarized, racialized, demonized, hidden, and inferiorized. At the same time, anything associated with Africa and her people is generally viewed through the race prism. The Afrocentric model of education, designed from an Afrocentric theoretical perspective, values African knowledge and offers a way to approach and dismantle racist views. It is an educational model that can teach everyone.

CHAPTER 7

The Need for an Afrocentric Education Model

I advance the Afrocentric Education Model to address the true nature of what we currently call "education," a term grounded in the establishment's desire to retain and remain in power. We may surmise that the conquered will always be "educated" to understand her, his, their, place in society. Henry Berry, Virginia House of Representatives, said in 1832[1]:

> We have, as far as possible, closed every avenue by which the light may enter the slave's mind. If we could extinguish the capacity to see the light, our work will be complete. They would then be on the level of the beast of the fields and we then should be safe. (Browder, 1992, p. 18)

This statement is representative of the racist thinking of politicians who owned and supported the enslavement of African people captured from the continent and brought to North America as animals. At the same time, the earlier Africans who traveled to the Americas thousands of years ago to settle in new lands across the world were also enslaved and genocide was committed against them to rid them of their lands and use their beautiful lands in the interests of the conquerors. While it is important to note that essentially these people were African in origin, they did not practice the ancient mother-centered or African matriarchal beliefs of their ancestors. In fact, they did not recognize their ancestors, those who lands they had stolen or those whom they captured and brought to the Americas—North, South, and Central. The reality is that all people in the United

---

[1]This quote is taken from Anthony Browder's *Nile Valley Contributions to Civilization: Exploding the Myths*. The Institute of Karmic Guidance, 1992. This is an important book that explains Kemet and can be used by anyone of any age. It has pictures and is easily readable.

States should be taught the true history of the United States to make sense of who we are and where we are and what we can become. At this time, the U.S. government led by President Trump is trying to bring back white supremacist thinking the doctrine within European cultural beliefs. The leadership of the U.S. government wishes to maintain the race paradigm and, in this way, go back to the way it was during enslavement when Black people had no power and could be murdered and lynched openly legally. The Governor of Florida believes that children should be protected from the truth, and yet, children are not protected from the harsh and true realities that some grow up in such as in the current situations with the Palestinian people of Gaza, the people of Congo, the Yemeni, and the Sudanese and even in the United States among the socially impoverished and those with no homes. These people have had amazing histories that have contributed to our human history. The First Nations children were not protected from truth when the conquerors came and destroyed everything that they held sacred. Enslaved African mothers and fathers had children born into enslavement, and European children attended the lynching of African women and men for entertainment. All the children were subjected to forms of barbarianism. What could be the explanation? Africology enables the investigation of the cultural history of humanity so that we may locate ourselves in the human story. In line with the thoughts regarding U.S. education, H. L. Menken (1880–1956) a scholar, journalist, commentator said:

> The aim of public education is not to spread enlightenment at all; it is simply to reduce as many individuals as possible to the same safe level, to breed and train a standardized citizenry, to put down dissent and originality. That is its aim in the United States, whatever the pretensions of politicians, pedagogues and other such mountebanks, and that is its aim everywhere else.[2]

In contrast, this pedagogical guide promotes the idea to young children that there are ethical and moral standards that all people once practiced regarding what it is to being or becoming human. It guides pupils to view the cultural potentiality of humanity. Pupils can logically understand that

---

[2]https://www.goodreads.com/quotes/435449-the-most-erroneous-assumption-is-to-the-effect-that-the

a culture that created a genetically falsely held belief in human inferiority and superiority is unwell. Does a sick culture need the medicine of truth to heal it? Will it die naturally from insanity? Is it even possible to make it well? While we ask these questions, we live in the now and it seems that the solution might be an intergenerational and intercultural project. DeSantis and the Supreme Court of Justice, so distant from its ancestor Maat the feminine divinity that gave us the earliest notions of Truth, Justice, Righteousness, Reciprocity, Harmony, Balance and Order want us to not be "woke", but we are already knowing. How could this idea take place? Would we be like the Sudra and Dalits, and our enslaved ancestors, forced to not read on the pain of death as they were? Are we talking progress or regress? Mwalimu Shujaa (1994) stated that[3]:

> [W]hile African Americans exist within the U.S. social context, they also exist within an African historical-cultural continuum that predates that social context and would continue to exist even if the nation state and its societal arrangements were to transform or demise. Schooling is a process intended to perpetuate and maintain the society's existing power relations and the institutional structures that support those arrangements ... Education in contrast to schooling, is the process of transmitting from one generation to the next, knowledge of the values, aesthetics, spiritual beliefs, and all things that give a particular cultural orientation its uniqueness ... Education and schooling processes are not mutually exclusive, they can overlap. There are aspects of schooling that can serve the common interests of all members of a society, regardless of their particular cultural orientations. (p. 15)

From the times of recorded conquests in Kemet, by the Hyksos, Assyrians, Persians, Greeks, Romans, Arabs, and Turks, African people have tried to transmit their sacred wisdom to their children. The conquests by Northern cradle practitioners with anti-African/Black religions have created havoc and had detrimental effects on populations for centuries, particularly those phenotypes of the darkest hue. Victims have attempted to recover from the carnage caused by those who came to conquer and installed their racist institutions to reflect their beliefs. In this way, academia, the brain of institutionalized racist cultural beliefs, has met with challenges

---

[3]Dr. Mwalimu Shujaa was the president of CIBI schools during the 1990s.

from the influx of representatives of the marginalized. The slow democratization or the process of Maaticity is occurring through the struggles of the descendants of enslaved Black/Africans with ancient, oriented minds, who are remembering, how life could or should be, in the continuing fight for human rights. Those of us with Southern cradle values have not accepted the Northern cradle beliefs in human rights as they are more or less nonexistent as history has shown us. More representatives of various phenotypes still have their African ancestral memories, which have awoken and will awake through knowledge—truth. Even in Kemet, Northern cradle conquests took place. For example, the sage, Ipuwer, possibly a witness to the Hyksos conquest in Kemet during 2130–1938 BCE, if we are to believe his words, and I for one do believe them, whether admonitions or lamentations:

> Lo, what the ancestors foretold has come to pass. The land is full of bands of evil-doers and the plowman goes to plow with his shield. Faces are pale, the bowman stand ready ... wrongdoing is everywhere and there is no man or woman of yesterday. Lo, the women are barren, and none can conceive, for God does not make children anymore because of the state of the land. There is blood everywhere and no shortage of the dead. Indeed, the burial cloth cries out before one approaches it. Lo, the land turns like a potter's wheel. The robber has become rich and the honorable person a thief. The foreigners from without have come to Kemet and the Kemite of yesterday cannot be found anywhere. (quoted in Karenga, 1984, p. 78)

In these ancient times in Africa, there were Northern cradle conquests taking place that ultimately led to the loss of Kemet and the whole of Africa to Arabia and Europe. During these conquests, the role of women and African matriarchal societies was slowly undermined by the conquerors. This is the state of Africa currently.

One can look on the map of Africa and see how each country has been created by conquerors to exploit the mineral wealth of these countries to furnish the conquerors' countries. Each newly created country was mapped out by Europeans in 1884 at the Berlin Conference. It served as a method to prevent Europeans continuing to war with each other for the wealth of Africa to build their homelands in Europe. The European first world war was mainly located in Africa with Europeans contending for lands and Africans forced to support these wars. This was the institution-alization of colonial governments. Early enslavement by Arabs was dated officially from the 7th century and then Europeans from 1400s, which included the enslavement and the genocide of the Taino and Carib led by Christopher Columbus in 1492 and the continuing genocide of the First Nations peoples across the Americas (Carew, 1994).

The taking of wealth is ongoing and the disputes among the *owners* of the lands continue until this day. The real owners are forced to "consider" *sovereignty of lands* created by colonizers. These contested European and Arab lands have disrupted and divided the traditional nations through religions and languages of the colonizers and enslavers. In the future, when Africa itself becomes sovereign, it will be a time when the resources of Africa will be used in the interests of its people, no longer entrapped in exploitative relations with anti-human, anti-African people who do not know themselves and their true humanitarian relations with their ancestors. This truism can be applied to the destruction of the first Africans who inhabit the Americas, and other parts of the world in Australia and the Pacific islands, etc. It was critically important over thousands of years that the knowledge of the African ancients was trans-ferred culturally to the descendants. Africology is the discipline that is discovering that we may learn of and pass on the ideas of the ancients upon whose knowledge many of the current ideas in the sciences, spiritu-ality, medicine, mathematics, architecture, education, astrology, astronomy, and music developed.

Families with Black children have learned that their children are nega-tively affected by educational resources that imply their inferiority in this learning process. This was the case in the UK when the children of Caribbean and African families were considered educationally subnormal from the 1960s until the 1980s. Their parents, who were literate and skilled, were invited to the country to fill the roles that Europeans did not have the skills or want to carry out. It was discovered that the children were sent to "special" schools as their parents arrived in the country off the ships. Many parents naturally thought their children, who were spe-cial to them, were entering "good" schools. The government policies were discovered to be at the foot of this outrage.

Bernard Coard (1971) from Grenada wrote a booklet called *How the West Indian Child is Made Educationally Sub-normal in the British School System*, which shook the UK's Black population. This reality inspired the foundation of Saturday schools or supplementary schools in major cities across the UK. The work of African/Black educationists particularly in the United States led by organizations like the Council of Independent Black Institutions (CIBI) has led the challenge against imposing inferiority-based information upon the children. Forced to acquiesce to such ideas as though they are true, all children will continue to grow up to understand their place in society, as explicated by Carter G. Woodson (1933a) when he said "The so-called modern education, with all its defects, however, does other so much more good than it does the Negro, because it has been worked out in conformity to the needs of those who have enslaved and oppressed weaker peoples. For example, the philosophy and ethics resulting from our educational system have justified slavery, peonage, segregation and lynching. The oppressor has the right to exploit, to handicap, and kill the oppressed … When you control a man's thinking you do not have to worry about his actions. You do not have to tell him not to stand here or go yonder. He will find his "proper" place and will stay in it. You do not have to send him to the back door. He will go without being told. In fact, if there is no back door, he will cut one for his special benefit. His education makes it necessary" (p. 4). The advancement or development of the Black person is viewed as part of the European anthropological racist idea of evolution. Culturally, within that discipline, African people are considered the least human and the idea of progress and development is based on the belief that becoming culturally European or psychologically "white" is the epitome of human development. Scientific evidence shows almost the opposite.

As Molefi Kete Asante (2017) explains:

> It is not alarmist to say that education, as a system, has not always been our friend; indeed, the statistics of the condition of African American education suggest that education has systematically robbed Black children of their motivation, creativity, cultural identity, and assertiveness. This means that children often leave school more damaged psychologically and culturally than they could have been or would have been had they remained at home. (p. ix)

The Afrocentric culturally oriented model of education is the attempt to deal with the reality that children are being trained in racist schools to learn who they are not, thus harming their potential to understand the beauty of their own humanity and how their beauty ties into the possibilities for all humanity. This is why I highlight human identity and emphasize that culture is the primary identity. With this truth, we are more able to begin a process of deconstructing racial beliefs that have been a major cause for human suffering, inequalities, hatred, divisions, insanity, murders, genocide, and wars. Furthermore, we may seek to nurture the concept of cultural unity as a basis for resolving imaginary differences and uplifting potential similitude.

The differences in treatment through forms of racism, the outcome of the practice and belief in race, is not denied or made invisible in this model. There is a focus on identifying racism and how it impacts our lives. The attempt to reveal the illogicity of the construction of race is to see the damage it has caused the world over and, in this way, work toward creating a future where it is possible to change the institutional structures that uphold its existence. These existing and future institutions would become culturally sensitive, Afrocentric. Through this model, by applying the standards of Maat, we can see that what happens to people victimized by anti-human behaviors is a problem of culture and humanity. The model is based on the idea that humans can change, institutions can change, and problems are solvable.

CHAPTER 8

Challenging Prevailing Racist Assumptions

I want the Afrocentric educator to see how differing cultures orient their notions of education to suit their needs. In North America, race predominates thus, and racist assertions and beliefs affect what we are taught and thus our visions of the past, the present, and the future.

- The Red race deservedly lost lands because they were considered savages unable to develop the full potential of their lands. Moreover, as primitives, they were poorly equipped to win the war for their lands. When they attempted to develop their lands, they were savages.

The reality is that First Nations people descended from ancient civilizations that were matriarchal, literate, and progressive, and that sought and succeeded in achieving democratic egalitarian ways of living. They developed cosmologies that respected nature and life; this is the essence of progressive. Moreover, we may understand the cultural similitude and continuity of their earlier African ancestors, for example, their calendar, their understanding of planetary movements, the building of pyramids, and the importance of women.

Based on the scientific reality that the first *Homo sapiens* were Africans, we can all connect our human ancestry to Africa. Dr. Imhotep (2021) traced the roots of First Nations people in North and South America, back to Africa, locating different migrations out of Africa. Africans in South America, 56,000 years ago in Brazil, and those in North America (South Carolina) 51,700 years ago are called Paleoamericans. They were Africans who possibly sailed directly from Africa. In this important work, the Dogon nation of Mali who were scientists at the time of Kemet were once Nile Valley inhabitants.[1] They were a Manding people like the Kemites. The Dogon people were also culturally related to the Hopi First nation people of Arizona in North America, one of the Pueblo nations, with their artifacts, clothing, masks, spiritual names, and dance, etc. These similarities were also seen among the Navaho and the Apache nations (Imhotep, 2021). Dr. Imhotep also found links between the Maya and Aztec people, who spoke of the Olmec people who came before them. The Olmec sailed to Mexico and introduced the calendar, government, religious teachings, and architectural styles. The Manding people formed the base of the Olmec and the Kushite people of Kemet. The age of these colossal stone heads in Mexico is dated from 680 to 800 BCE. This timing correlates to the 25th Dynasty of Kemet and the possibility of a maritime connection. Below are depictions of the Olmec Colossal stone head carvings, 17 of which have been discovered. The heads range from 1.8 to 3 m in height.

The Olmecs existed more than 10,000 BCE. According to Imhotep (2021, p. 112), "they began thousands of years before they morphed into the Mayans, whom we phenotypically understand as First nations people." Below is the Mayan Pyramid of Chiapas in Mexico that has writing embellished in it. Below that is one of the paintings at the top of the pyramid inside. You can see that the Mayans have dark skin advancing the idea of their African origin.

---

[1]The Dogon people of Mali are of African nation who lived contemporaneously at the time of Kemet; they are known to have located a dwarf planet known as Sirius B centuries before Europeans with massive telescopes discovered it.

There were pyramid builders in Central America, with accomplishments such as the Pyramids of the Sun and the Moon complex; temple pyramid builders in South America, as in the Tiahuanaco and Peru; and the civilization the Bahamas and Caribbean before the Ice age-ending cataclysmic melt/flood wiped them out (Imhotep, 2021, p. 113).

The First Nations People of the Americas Fought Valiantly and were Murdered Relentlessly.

- Land ownership by the "white race" was natural, as the white race was the most able to develop land. The white race was civilized and thus better equipped intellectually and militarily to conquer the red race.

The reality is that the Europeans who traversed the world and sought lands and wealth, by any means necessary, used their profits from the wealth of the people whom they conquered to create weaponry that would guarantee a faster way of achieving conquest, using the lands and people to develop their own industries through brutality and fear. When Christopher Columbus' flagship the Santa Maria ran aground on the island of modern-day Haiti and the Dominican Republic, which he called Hispaniola, the Taino people led by their King Waka Nagari took their boats that held as many as 150 rowers and helped save the ship's belongings.

Columbus was invited onto the island and was amazed and grateful. He thought Taino life was wonderful (Carew, 1994).[2] He wrote in his diary that there were neither better people nor land, and the houses and villages were so pretty. They love their neighbors as themselves, they have the sweetest speech in the world, and they are gentle and always laughing.

Waka Nagari was a regional King, and five kings were his subjects. Columbus gave Waka Nagari a red hat and Waka Nagari gave him a golden crown. To Waka Nagari, the hat was a gift. To Christopher Columbus, the crown symbolized the entitlement to the lands and people of Waka Nagari. He told Spain of wealth, that the people are naked without weapons, and that he can subdue the island. He had a fort built on the island and left for Spain. He returned with seven armed ships and began the slaughter of the indigenous people, including their Queen Anacaona, and the conquest of the Caribbean (Carew, 1994).

In this conquering process that took hundreds of years, an important part of the conquest of the First Nations people in North America was to take the children from their families. In the early 1800s, this was the government policy for indigenous people while at the same time the enslavement of African people was taking place. The remaining original keepers of the lands, it was believed, needed to become culturally white or European or acculturated. The process of imposing European culture upon the children from as young as 4 years old was to send the children to boarding schools far away from their homes. This barbarous idea was to civilize the supposedly uncivilized. The atrocities committed were hidden until more recently when the voice of the First Nations people could be heard. Regarding "education" as earlier explicated, this institutional process will always develop in line with the cultural beliefs of the institution builders (NBC News, 2022). There were hundreds of schools involved in this anti-indigenous movement, and it has been conservatively estimated that 100,000 children were ripped from their families and 40,000 children died as a result. The schooling process is a critical part of the genocide process for the First Nations people. In the following YouTube video, Braveheart, a Lakota nation victim, speaks of his experiences and the teachings of his wise mother, who told him in relation to those who committed

---

[2]Jan Carew's book is a great reference for the story of Columbus.

these atrocities "the accountability is to let the divine take care of that": https://www.google.com/url?q=https://www.youtube.com/watch?v%3Dp cAZsf96d3U&sa=D&source=docs&ust=1754265398150986&usg=AOv Vaw12eRzSWEuybhBa8BN9z48E

- The enslavement of the Black race by European and Arab cultures is based on the inferiority of Black people, who were viewed as sinners, animals, and subhumans, yet peace loving and acceptable of this status. Enslavement was/is still practiced in places like Libya, Mauritania, Sudan, Niger, Chad, as a desirable economical method of exploiting energies while civilizing Black people.

Yet, as Chancellor Williams (1987) explicated:

Ghana's actual history goes far back beyond its known record. That record list forty-four kings before the Christian era, and this alone would extend Ghana's known history beyond the 25th Dynasty when the last Black pharaohs ruled Egypt (7th century BC) ... it nevertheless reached a high level of greatness in the eleventh century and was an empire comparable to most European states at that time. It surpassed many others in social organization, military power, economic wealth and in the promotion of higher education ... The empire, known as the "Land of Gold" became great not only because it controlled the greatest resource of gold for both Europe and Asia, but also because of its iron mining and iron manufactures for over a thousand years ... There were import and export taxes, a system of weights and measures, and control of inflation by limiting the flow of gold. Kumbi-Kumbi, the capital, was a twin city of stone mansions, temples, mosques and schools, along with the thatched-roof huts of the masses. (p. 197)

The people of Ghana allowed others to live in peace with them, hence the mosques standing next to their temples, etc. The reality is that African/ Black people are not inferior and came from civilizations that were matriarchal, egalitarian, scientific, democratic, and wealthy. There was no need to civilize those who were already civilized. The capitalist method of enslavement, and the immeasurable, unquantifiable profits, made Europeans the most militarily powerful people in the world. The belief in the race paradigm based on the contrived immorality of the African/

Black woman and man justified Arabian enslavement and continues to create wealth for Islam even in places like Saudi Arabia. These methods of chattel enslavement cost and still cost the loss of millions of African lives.

- The white race is the most genetically evolved intelligent group with the natural (God given) authority to rule and develop other races.

Chronology and science show that genetically the white race is not a race, but instead a collection of phenotypes with less melanin. Humans left Africa as *Homo sapiens*, melaninated Africans, and some lived in a land mass now called Europe. As evidence of an ancient European, whose full skeleton was found in a cave in Devon in England called the Cheddar Cave. He is known as Cheddar man and is 9 to 10,000 years old. He has blue eyes.

The first people to populate Europe were dark skin Africans. They were estimated to have arrived 40,000 years ago, possibly more as archaeologists do not have set times for dating. They were the ancestors of the less melaninated phenotypes who developed to accommodate surviving in colder climates where it is less healthy for survival to have an abundance of melanin in the skin. There is melanin in our vital organs, so all humans have melanin. Importantly, people mix all the time, resulting in differing phenotypical colors, mixed into a variety of shades as they came and went traveling to different parts of the world. Importantly, melanin does not denote whether a person is good or bad, although there can be preferences in the cultures that can be associated with certain melanin colors. In the development of white supremacy, the construction of race, those who are privileged by this cultural and social construct have more interest in believing in it and gravitating toward those who benefit like them. However, in this Afrocentric model of education from an African matriarchal perspective, there is the reality that we all have Black African ancestors.

The key to understanding our cultural identity is to know what culture is. Culture transmits knowledge intergenerationally and is a reservoir or repository of the memories of our journey as *Homo sapiens* out of Africa and remaining in Africa. In this light, there are people with less melanin who retain the memory of some of the ancient values and beliefs of their Black African ancestors.

Culture can be learned and can be more unifying in bringing people together than the falsehood of race, which succeeds in dividing humanity. Some of us become embroiled in the culture of hatred, division, and war, and this way of being becomes acceptable over time and visions of change become unrealistic. We then resort to believing that genetics dictates our ability to change when they are associated with notions of inferiority and superiority.

The early arrivals of Africans to Europe are anthropologically and archaeologically contested, as the construction of race has made it extremely difficult to provide praise and excellence by European standards relating to Black people who have been constructed as inferior, uncivilized, and backward. The work requires a truth that is difficult to grapple with when lies and fantasy have been upheld as truth. Early African people to Europe have been sometimes called the Grimaldi ("Grimaldi Man," n.d.). Grimaldi is the name given to the African bones found in a cave in Italy in 1901 that are possibly 26,000 to 47,000 years old. Prince Albert I, of the Grimaldi family of Monaco, financed and gave his name to the exploration of seven caves, hence the name Grimaldi Africans, early Europeans. So much is hidden and disguised that one becomes mystified and remains mystified. We still refer to Grimaldi Africans who are just Africans or *Homo sapiens* with dark skins.

The research of Scottish Historian David MacRitchie (1991) shows evidence of early African migrations. Based on linguistics and clan names of those deemed Scottish, a changeable status, he identifies Black/African people, like the Black Danes and clans or characters like Douglas, McLeod, and Campbell, revealing differing ethnicities, their relations, some positive, some negative. He identifies the root languages of words and grounds some of the prevailing ideas into a semblance of truth with knowledge that race, and racism influence important methods of translation. White supremacy still pervades the perspectives of historians.

MacRitchie makes important inroads into forgotten, buried but relevant histories. In some British Coats of Arms or Family Crests, there are signs and symbols relating to Black people, women and men who are not enslaved but rather royal. David MacRitchie's research showed some evidence of early families that held rulership over areas in the British Isles, now known as the UK. Below are interesting pictures of some of the crests, which signify the Brocas family members (possibly from 1300s) of the royal families in Britain who would rather not remember. Clearly, these pictures show Black African women and men in royal positions.

Brocas family of UK possibly 1300s

Importantly and rarely discussed in the subject of the hatred and disrespect of the Black people of the world, are the indigenous Australians, called First Nations people who populated the land now known as Australia and surrounding islands. The First Nations people of Australia left Africa around 72,000 years ago, according to research of the first genome study of the indigenous population (ABC News (Australia), 2011; Malaspinas et al., 2016). The genocide of the First Nations people of Australia by Europeans who practiced the doctrine of white supremacy had gone unchallenged until recently. Prior to the 1967 referendum, indigenous First Nations people of Australia and the Torres Strait Islands were not counted toward Australia's population, as they were not considered citizens. The original people were often hunted like animals and killed as a pastime for white supremacists until recently, I remember young white Australians coming to Earls Court in London, UK, in the 1960s and

1970s speaking of the hunting of the First Nations people as a pastime. Hunters would go out in the jeeps with a headlight and search for traces of First Nations people hiding away from danger and shoot them. I never knew what these people did with the bodies of their victims and whether they took trophies as the lynch mobs in the United States did. Today, the First Nations people of Australia and the Torres Strait Island represent only 3.2% of the Australian population. Below a woman from the Torres Strait Island and a First Nations family are shown.

The children were taught through culture antithetical to their humanity, to reject their First Nations culture as well as their own Black beauty.

It is imperative to understand the purposeful whitening of Australian indigenous people by cruelly and forcibly removing over 100,000 children from their families. The process of whitening is under the guise of civilizing. The belief in white supremacy asserts that the whiter one is, or the less melanin one has, including the families who have albinism, the lack of melanin in their skin when they are born into dark skin families often living in hot climates that put their health and survival in danger: The more civilized one is. The Half-caste Act of Victoria 1886 in Australia gave the government permission to remove children from their families because they were the progeny of the children of First Nations people and Europeans.

It was believed that their European look or light skin was a sign of a more civilized human, and the plan was to remove the children and train them how to become civilized by taking them out of the First Nations' peoples' communities. This removal caused great sadness and depression as the children were violently taken from their families and lost their culture. The First Nations people of Australia do not recognize "race" as part of their culture. Their culture is African matriarchal in orientation. The lighter skin children were called the "stolen generation." The children were fostered, put in homes, and sent to white families to begin the process of whitening." They and their original parents could not recover from such trauma.

They were taught through culture antithetical to their humanity, to reject their First Nations' culture as well as their own Black beauty. The policy of assimilation was the attempt to deculturalize First Nations people through the prevention of practicing their cultural values and beliefs by making their values and behaviors appear barbarous and uncivilized in the fashion of the treatment of the First Nations people in the Americas and the descendants of enslaved Black Africans in the United States. The assimilation policy operated from the 1800s to the 1970s. According to Fiona Probyn-Rapsey (2013, p. x):

> Most members of the Stolen Generations had white fathers or grandfathers. Who were these white men? This book analyses the stories of white fathers, men who were positioned as key players in the plans to assimilate Aboriginal people by "breeding out the colour." The policy of breeding out the colour was a cruel farce. It conflated skin colour with culture and assumed that Aboriginal women and their children would acquiesce to produce "future whites." It also assumed that white men would comply as ready appendages, administering "whiteness" through marriage or white sperm.

As planned, descendants of the stolen generation have light skin and can pass as white. What was unforeseen was that many remembered their families and came to know their culture and respect their ancient ancestors. They remain faithful to their people's values and beliefs and stand in defiance of the murdering and debasement of their dark skin families. This is in some ways a similar situation to the United States, whereby on the one hand many of those who can pass for white become anti-Black in their beliefs in support of white supremacy. While on the other hand, there are those who can pass for white but stand in support of their African ancestry and their dark skin families. In this sense with the application of the race paradigm, those appearing white who support Black struggle are not recognized as pro-Black or Black in a conscious way.

Moreover, the acculturation policy to whiten the primitive in Australia is one that can be likened to the government's process of taking the children of the indigenous people of North America from their homes and sending them to boarding schools where many of them died. The Afrocentric educator knows that it is possible, regardless of the belief in the falsehood of "race" to connect or reconnect with our ancestors and the ancient traditions. For pictures of current demonstrations on the streets against policies that still take First Nations children out of their families called "Out of Home Care" policy (Knowles, 2020), please refer to the photographs.

Tyson Yunkaporta (2019), from the Apalech clan, a Wik Mungkan speaker, who wrote *sand talk: How Indigenous Thinking Can Save the World*, asks us to respect:

> The Elders and traditional custodians of the land and other beings everywhere who keep the Law of the Land. The Ancestors, the old people from every People now living on the continent and its islands. Our non-human kin, including the various spiky species around the world, the porcupines and hedgehogs who snuffle in the earth for ants and then do God knows what when we're not looking. I don't know why Stephen Hawking and others have worried about super intelligent beings from other planets coming here and using their advanced knowledge to the world what industrial civilization has already done. Beings of higher intelligence are already here, always have been. They just haven't used the intelligence to destroy anything yet. Maybe they will if they tire of the incompetence of domesticated humans. (p. 2)

The important idea is that the First Nations writer is speaking for his people, wrongly disrespected and removed genocidally from their lands. It is they who are people of high learning, not those who committed the crimes against them. This truth may be said to be the case of humans who are in touch with their environment and know how to live in it with respect. They are practicing Maat. Their Black ancestors and the elders are the *wisdom keepers* who maintain the cultural transmission of truth and knowledge in spite of genocide. In 2017, the First Nations people came together to make a statement regarding the sacred red rock of Uluru. Please refer to the photographs to see the beautiful sacred red rock of Uluru.

Two hundred indigenous representatives from across the country came to look at how "Aboriginal" and Torres Strait Islander people could be recognized in the Constitution to have a Voice in Parliament ("Uluru statement from the heart," 2017).[3]

> We gathered at the 2017 National Constitutional Convention, coming from all points of the southern sky, make the statement that sovereignty is a spiritual notion: The ancestral tie between the land, or "mother nature," and the Aboriginal and Torres Strait Islander peoples who were born therefrom, remain attached thereto, and must one day return thither to be united with our ancestors. The link is the basis of the ownership of the soil, or, better, of sovereignty. It has never been ceded or extinguished and co-exists with the sovereignty of the crown.

This statement was to take ownership of this red sacred stone and stop tourists and non-indigenous people from climbing it and disrespecting its spiritual sacredness and value to people all over Australia. Below is a picture of Uluru. In life, it is so beautiful that no picture can present the reality of its beauty or sacredness.

Africa has more phenotypes than any other continent. Differing phenotypes left Africa and became the people of today. The stereotype of Africans who left Africa has caused many problems for archaeologists and anthropologists who are guilty of creating notions of skeletal types in the desire to create human divisions in the race construction. The Khoisan

---

[3]You can view and hear the statement at https://ulurustatement.org/the-statement/view-the-statement/

people, sometimes Khoi and San, have been labeled by racists as Bushmen in relation to their closeness with nature and/or Hottentots in relation to the click language spoken. These racist terms have become normalized.

Charles Darwin "wrote about a future time when the gap between human and ape will increase by the anticipated extinction of such intermediates as chimpanzees and Hottentots" (Gould, 1981, p. 36). In other words, the Khoisan people were considered intermediaries between apes and humans (Online Media TV, 2018). These lies parading as academic truths have affected the life changes in the Khoisan people so deleteriously that today in South Africa, they have had their culture and lands taken and been forced to live as "coloreds" when they are an African phenotype, one of the most ancient (Isaacson, 2002). During the conquest of South Africa, the Khoisan people were murdered to clear the lands, many went into the Kalahari Desert to survive the rigors of barbarism. Even in the desert where diamonds were found, the Khoisan were rounded up and removed. They were hunted for sport by the white Afrikaners, much like the First Nations people of Australia. The Khoisan people in South Africa number only 100,000. As mentioned in the book *The Afrocentric School [a blueprint]* (Dove, 2021), far from being intermediaries between humans and apes, these people were scientists who tracked the movements of the planets to record the menses of the women. These women scientists should be heralded the Lebombo bone, 45,000-year-old evidence of this astrological and mathematical knowledge. It takes thousands of years to track the movements of the sun and moon and planets. Below is a picture of a Khoisan family, although it is important to remember that the Khoisan people work in all walks of life, but always try to maintain their cultural beliefs. Some tracing the phenotypes across the world see the likeness of the Khoisan people, to the later Chinese people who recognize their African origin.

The people of Papua New Guinea often have blonde hair as do some of the First Nations people in Australia. Below are pictures of members of nations of Papua New Guinea. They are not considered African and rarely mentioned in any cultural history of the people who left Africa and populated the world, or in terms of those who run their country.

In 1976, then Foreign Minister Ben Tanggahma was questioned regarding the political situation with Papua New Guinea (Maglangbayan & Moore, 1976):

Question: Minister, in the past few months the major world's news media have reported largescale fighting going on in the Southeast Asia Pacific region between the Republic of Indonesia on the one hand, and on the other, the guerilla forces of the Democratic Government of West Papua New Guinea.

Answer: Yes, but the press fails to inform people about the fact that these are struggles in which poor, disinherited Black populations—both in East Timor and West Papua New Guinea—are fighting against a yellow supremacist, racist, expansionist, colonialist and fascist empire: the Republic of Indonesia.

Question: It is a fact that even in the United States, where people are supposedly in possession of the greatest amount of information about what is going on in the world, there is great ignorance about your struggles. And certainly, it was only recently that most people in the U.S.A. were informed even that Black peoples were living in those areas of Asia.

Answer: Yes, that is true. Nevertheless, Black peoples have been inhabiting all regions of Asia for many thousands of years. In fact, the aboriginal populations of Southern China and the entire Southeast Asia (the Philippines, Kampuchea, Laos, Vietnam, Malaysia, Burma,

Thailand and Indonesia) were Black. Black populations are still in the jungle areas of those nations even today, though living as marginal peoples and facing many hardships in most cases.

Question: The Black peoples of the islands of New Guinea and Timor, who are now fighting the Indonesians, are therefore part of that great belt of aboriginal Black populations that settled in Asia?

Answer: Yes. We on the island of New Guinea and on the island of Timor belong to what is known as Melanesia, or Black Islands, if we translate it literally.

Before getting in the political particulars of your struggle, let us address West Papua New Guinea.

Question: What is your relationship toward Africa and Africans?

Answer: Africa is our motherland. All of the Black populations which settled in Asia over the hundreds of thousands of years came undoubtedly from the African continent. In fact, the entire world was populated from Africa. Hence, we the Blacks in Asia and the Pacific today descend from proto-African peoples. We were linked to Africa in the Past. We are linked to Africa in the future. We are what you might call the Black Asian Diaspora.

When questioned about colonization, the minister said, Papua New Guinea is the most colonized place on the earth.

For books on this kind of information, the works of Ivan Van Sertima who recognized the African origin of humanity and his researchers, colleagues who seek the *African presence* in all the countries of the world offer an immeasurable wealth of knowledge. Using the Afrocentric Education Model enables educators and pupils to connect to other Black people in the world who are descendants of Africa. In this way, we can locate many of the cultural histories that we, as teachers and learners, might become interested in as part of curriculum development and personal development.

The African origin of Chinese people is known by Chinese scientists ("African History Fountain," 2023; "Black Journals," 2023; "The African Origins of China: The Genographic Project," 2023). Please look at the photographs of the Black Chinese people. In 2005, the National Geographic Society and IBM launched a genetic anthropology study to map human migrations from Africa by analyzing DNA samples. The principal investigator, Professor Jin Li at the National Human Genome Center and the president of Fudan's University in Shanghai, found evidence that most of the gene pools in China originated from Africa. Some see a connection of the Chinese people to their possible ancestors, the Khoisan people.

Another little-known Black people indigenous the Philippines are the Aeta. There is a photograph below. The Aeta are mentioned above by the Foreign Minister of Papua New Guinea Ben Tanggahma in his interview by Shawna Maglangbayan and Carlos Moore, when speaking of the Black/African people of Southeast Asia, of whom we must learn so more of.

The journeys of African migrations out of Africa are being located in the story of humanity. The differences seem so vast and varied. As locations are found and cultural differences and similarities are identified, Diop's assertion that the power relationships between the woman and the man are the foundation as the development of culture becomes relevant when investigating the cultural orientation of a people. It is possible to assess the level of societal enlightenment in the civilization in relation to the position and status of the mother (Dove, 2002). Because of the dislocation from our ancestors in the Southern cradle, some Africans forgot their ancestors and created a racist patriarchy controlled by an elite. Patriarchy and racism go hand in hand. Part of the process of reconnecting to cultural history, legacy, and memory is incumbent on creating a pedagogy inclusive of environments in which the ideas are learned, and reciprocity is highlighted as the basis for discussion and learning among people.

The cultural importance of African/Black women is to be exemplified for balance and harmony. This is why culture is so critical. This idea is not based solely on biological difference, but on what is a woman and what is a man. It is the culture created by the mind of people that influences the ways that people work together.

CHAPTER 9

Cultural Memory and the Significance of African Matriarchy

The egalitarian status between women and men was/is perceived by patri-archs to be a state of barbarism in an evolutionary process of becoming civilized. From a European anthropological point of view, patriarchy, the domination of the woman by the man is viewed culturally and histori-cally as the beginning of civilization. This belief relates the conquests across the world of the Black/African societies whose wealth has been stolen and the people exploited. The further back anthropologists, archaeologists, and historians go in studying and examining human his-tory, the more evidence there is to show African matriarchy existed, all over the world. The further back they go, the more African *Homo sapiens* are found populating the world. From an Afrocentric perspective, this is logical as life began in Africa and waves of African people of all genders and phenotypes left Africa around 50 to 70,000 years ago to venture into their new world with the intelligence, knowledge, and tools for survival.

The act of dominating the woman is the first injustice, hierarchy, and act of barbarism. We may say this condition is based on lack of trust, jeal-ousy, and the need to control, if trying to build logic into the modern religions. Although patriarchy still predominates globally, there is still evidence in differing parts of the world that African matriarchy still exists in a deep cultural structure. In other words, although patriarchy has been imposed as an institutional system of domination, from relationships, family, religions, education, health care, politics, governance, economics, and entertainment, the memories and institutional evidence of the past remain embedded culturally in old traditions, values, beliefs, behaviors, some practiced in secret, some remembered and commemorated. As Africologists, educators and truth-seekers, our work in providing the his-torical, cultural knowledge of past beliefs, behaviors, values, traditions, and achievements is to help us remember the past and become conscious of the possibilities of a different future.

The process of remembering history is called Sankofa. Sankofa is a masculine divinity of history in the Akan (a federation of nations in Ghana) spiritual system. The idea of Sankofa is that one must take the best ideas of the past and use them to build and create a future. It literally means "go back and fetch it." The Sankofa is symbolized by a bird looking backward and holding the egg of knowledge (or the sphere of the world) for the future, gained from its historical search in the past. Below is the image of the Sankofa bird.

An important part of remembering is the connection with ancestors. We remember those who came before and upon whose shoulders we stand. We thank them for all they have done for us. As noted earlier, there are only good ancestors, those who have done their best to improve life. Those are the ones whom we remember and give reverence to. Part of the process of cultural dislocation, domination, and imperialism has been to forbid revering ancestors who are the good people who made the world a better place in the smallest and largest of ways. This condition of cultural dislocation through cultural imposition and forced forgetting has been a critical part of cultural domination. We have forgotten the ancient past and thus who we are. We now practice Sankofa by using the Afrocentric Education Model as a tool for research and discovery building knowledge—truth to access memory.

WHAT HAPPENED TO THE WOMAN, THE MOTHER OF HUMANITY?

In any culture, as stated earlier, institutions uphold societies and, of necessity, reflect the cultural values and beliefs of their creators. Thus, any culture that believes in and practices patriarchy and racism, the society and its institutions will reflect those beliefs. That is why in the United States, for example, the statistics for maternal mortality rates for non-Hispanic Black (subsequently, Black) women in 2001 were 69.9 deaths per 100,000 live births, 2.6 times the rate for non-Hispanic white (subsequently, white) women (Hoyert, 2023). In 2022, infant mortality rate for non-Hispanic Blacks/African Americans was 2.4 times than that for non-Hispanic whites (Centers for Disease Control [CDC], 2024b, Table 2).

- Non-Hispanic Black/African American infants are almost four times as likely to die from complications related to low birth weight as compared with non-Hispanic white infants (CDC, 2024b, Table 4).
- In 2020, non-Hispanic Black/African American infants had 2.9 times the sudden infant death syndrome mortality rate as non-Hispanic whites (Centers for Disease Control [CDC], 2024a, Tables 13 and 14).
- In 2020, non-Hispanic Black/African American mothers were twice as likely to receive late or no prenatal care as compared to non-Hispanic white mothers (CDC, 2024a, Tables 13 and 14).

The United States jails more women than Russia, China, Thailand, and India combined. Nearly a third of the world's female inmates are incarcerated in the United States. In the United States, 1 in 111 white women stands a likelihood of imprisonment in her lifetime. Latinas can expect that 1 in 45 will be imprisoned in her lifetime; and for African American women, the numbers are 1 in 18, who will probably experience incarceration. The current population of women in U.S. prisons is 201,200, and some of them are mothers and some will have and have had their babies in prison (Goodwin, 2020b). From a white supremacist position, this is perceived as justice, the women deserve to be there, and that is why they are there. From a Black/African perspective, this is racism and patriarchy combined.

Logically, from the Afrocentric perspective, historically and culturally, the first injustice was against the woman and is reflected in the societies that arose from patriarchal domination. The concept of justice that existed for thousands of years was removed from the patriarchal cultural orientation. The African woman and the African man have been debased, demeaned, inferiorized, demonized, and injured deeply. The notion of justice exists in the cultural memory of the legacy and achievements of African people, which means all people as we are all from the same motherland and linked by our mitochondrial DNA to one Black/African mother. Somewhere in the mythology of time, when African/Black people in the United States struggle for justice, the standard of justice is based on the ancient principles of Maat, which all humanity has a distant awareness of as Maat is the first understanding that we have codified of a moral order inclusive of Justice, Truth, Righteousness, Reciprocity, Humanity, Balance, Order. Maat sits even today on the roof of the Old Bailey in London as a symbol of justice. Below is a photograph of Lady Justice who sits on top of the Law Courts of the Old Bailey in London. Lady Justice is a copy of Maat. She represents Northern cradle justice holding the scales that symbolize the heart being weighed against Maat's feather of truth. Lady Justice wields a sword symbolizing the power of justice. If the heart is heavier than the Maat's feather of truth, Ammit will devour it. The life being judged is literally in her hands. Unlike Maat, this justice is limited to human laws of patriarchy and race.

It is possible to identify Maatic principles in the major religions. Ironically, the struggles of African/Black people moved the United States toward something called democracy, which in its divine form is effectively, Maat. In patriarchy, it is clearly more of a dream, speech, and literature than a reality. The irony is that Maat is ancient and lost in the mists of time and yet in the theory of evolution; the past was of a barbaric nature, and we are progressing toward becoming civilized. The woman is still not equal to the man in the present. Maat still does not exist in her fullness. How is this possible if we are progressing as the story of evolution proposes?

ARE WE PROGRESSING?

Ancient paintings from rocks and caves have been found that are as much as 73,000 years old and some reveal African women and men working together all over the world in hunting, farming, and animal rearing, and so on. These images may be found in the photographs. They are records in symbols painted at the time of these powerful events. The fact that these paintings are symbols, what we call writing that have lasted for thousands of years is a testament to the artists' and authors' scientific knowledge necessary to depict and sustain as a critical part of the restoration of cultural memory. There are dates of some of the beautiful paintings. More recently, it has been suggested that women may have created many of these ancient paintings.[1] We can align this thought with the Lebombo bone marked to represent the movement of the planets, in particular the moon in relation to women's menses. In this way, we can conceive of women as scientists.

44,000 BCE

28,000–30,000 BCE

---

[1] By comparing the relative lengths of fingers in the eight caves in France and Spain, archaeologist Dean Snow from Pennsylvania State University determined that three-quarters of the handprints were of females.

10,000 BCE

So far, we can say that the early written and codified evidence of the women's importance, rulership in society, is from the chronology (a calendar of events) listing Queen Neith-Hotep 5581 BCE of the first dynasty of Kemet. Her name signifies her respect for the divinity of Neith, who is known as mistress of the bow, whose antiquity places her in the time of Ta Seti, which means land of the bow, a pre-Kemetic, Kushite/Nubian society that was dynastic as evidenced by Professor Bruce Williams from Chicago who found a dynastic incense burner in Qustul in Ta Seti Kush proving that Ta Seti as a dynastic society existed before Kemet and may will have been instrumental in the building of Kemet. This chronology provided by the priest Manetho was commissioned by the Greek Pharaoh Ptolemy II, also known as Philadelphus. The priest Manetho was asked to provide a true chronology of the rule of the African *Per aa* before Greek conquest. The priest Manetho's dating is earlier than the "official" Egyptological timeline of 3200 BCE. Manetho begins Kemet's chronology 2,500 years earlier, beginning in 5717 BCE. This timeline has led to contention among Egyptologists who ignore this dating for reasons still to be uncovered. A timeline will be included to help in the chronological placing of some important events that may be built up.

Dove (2002) argued that the invasions of Kemet by the Hyksos, Assyrians, Persians, Greeks, Romans, Arabians, and Turkish were patriarchal and undermined the African Matriarchy of Kemet. Dove asserts that Kemet was founded on a mother-centered matrix that was central to the development of all African societies. These foreign conquests attempted to quash the power of women. Marriage into the African royal families led to the erosion of the women's power as foreigners aligned themselves to their fathers. The resurgence of the Mother-Centered Matrix was regenerated by the Kushite Kings and Queens of Kemet's 25th Dynasty in 750 to 675 BCE. Kushite Queens or Kandakes were inducted into leadership positions in Kemet and ruled for nearly 100 years before the coming of the conquering Assyrians (a nation within Mesopotamia) and Persians (Iranians).

Women in Kemet, as well as being leaders and politicians, were important socially, in everyday life, in every institution from family, health care, spirituality, governance, sciences, writing, education, economics, farming, weaving, the arts, and entertainment. Women had their own entitlements to their belongings, from children to their family heirlooms, furniture, pots, artifacts, lands, etc., and their rights were embedded in law (Lesko, 1996). Law was the domain of Maat, who was the ultimate judge for justice. Women's rights were re-empowered during the 25th Dynasty of Kush. As Barbara Lesko (1996) informs us:

> Four thousand years ago the women of Egypt enjoyed more legal rights and privileges than women have in many nations of today's world. Equal pay for equal work is a cry heard now but was practiced thousands of years ago in Egypt (Kemet) Whether as an employee of the State, a vendor in the marketplace, the manager of a household, or as an active participant among the clergy in the religious hierarchies, the ancient Egyptian (Kemite) held a vital place in her society that amazed and bewildered foreign contemporaries who observed her. (p. 1)

The Kushites Kings and Queens worked side by side. The Queens, known as Kandake or Kandaces, took important political positions as high priestesses with their own prime ministers who were women and men. They created building restorations and public works. It was a high point in Kemet's development (possibly the last).

The Kings and Kandakes (high priests and priestesses) ruled Kemet from their own governing centers in Meroe and Napata in Kush. Kush had played a role in Kemetic rulership over the years. During the Roman conquest of Kemet from 30 BCE to 323 ACE, the Kushite royalty, defended Kush/Nubia from Roman incursion. After the Romans had taken Kemet KMT, including land belonging to Kush, Kandake Amanirenas entered the occupied territory, attacked towns, and destroyed statues of Caesar. A Roman soldier blinded her in one eye. In retaliation, the Romans attacked Kush and burned Napata but failed to capture the Kandake Amanirenas. Realizing his vulnerability, Petronius, the prefect of Roman Egypt, fortified their occupation of Premnis in Kush and returned to Alexandria. Kandake Amanirenas marched again to secure her land. Petronius returned. As these armies stood face to face, they came to a political agreement that involved Caesar, who agreed to withdraw the troops from Kush.

Please refer to the photographs to see the images of Amanirenas who fought the Romans successfully from 23 to 21 BCE and a golden bejeweled bracelet that she wore. The Kandakes, as well as soldiers-warriors, rulers, spiritual leaders were mothers, wives, and family oriented. The reverence for women, in particular mothers, is not held in patriarchal societies. Respect for women may be written and spoken, but the societies will show the truth of social status regarding where women are placed in societal institutions from family to governance, economies, religion, and so on. Kush was later conquered by the Arabian people when they conquered Kemet in 651 ACE after the Romans. Ta Seti Kush is today's Sudan. Sudan is recognized by its Arabized Africans as the land of Blacks or the land of slaves.

Kandake Amanirenas

It should be noted that Per aa Cleopatra VII, the last ruler before the Roman conquest of Kemet, was the daughter of the Greek dynasty of

Ptolemy 332 to 30 BCE. Cleopatra VII was culturally African and fought the Romans during their maritime civil war at Actium 32 to 30 BCE. As a Kemetic queen, she supported the Roman General, Marc Anthony, with her troops against the Romans led by Octavian. Marc Anthony lost and Cleopatra VII lost Kemet in 30 BCE to the Romans, and the Kemites became Rome's colonial subjects. On one of my journeys to Kemet, I saw the Temple of Het-Her, or Hathor the Greek name, and marveled at its beauty. It had been built by Cleopatra 7th in honor of the divine Het-Her the mother and healer. There existed a far older temple for Het-Her below it. It was evident that she was culturally African. Women from all over the world wandered in and sat in and pondered in this temple as if drawn to it knowing that it was for the great mother. The Romans tried to continue their imperialism to conquer Kush from 25 to 21 BCE. Amanirenas and her armies fought the Romans who agreed to a peace treaty.

The following collections of photographs represent Cleopatra who was a mother and then the divine mothers of Het-Her, Auset, Mut, Sekhmet, and Neith. These divine mothers were critically important to the spiritual protection and safety of the Per aa women or men and thus Kemet.

Cleopatra VII

Divine Mothers

Het-Her   Auset   Mut   Sekhmet   Neith

CHAPTER 10

The Writer's Motive

The first book that I wrote was on African mothers in the United Kingdom and the United States, who wished to create Saturday schools that focused on the children learning their African history and heritage. The book was called *Afrikan Mothers, Bearers of Culture: Makers of Social Change*. It was grounded in the experiences of the beautiful activist women whom I was privileged to meet and whom I came to know, who entrusted me with their stories and allowed me to publish some very sensitive thoughts and experiences to encourage other mothers to seek the truth of the African experience for their children to learn. They knew me from the work we did together in the establishment of the schools that were part-time in the United Kingdom and full-time in the United States. I used Cheikh Anta Diop's two-cradle theory to understand the debasement of African women, in particular the Black mother as it was that most women in this movement were mothers. I explain the motive for writing this book and being a guide, as I came late to enter the world of academic thought, a position that I did not foresee at the time I met the first UK mothers. Now as an Africologist trained in Afrocentric metatheory that I have contributed to as an African womanist, an objective is to make clear the influence of cultural orientation in Afrocentric education, in the hope that as both teach and learner, some ideas will be useful to the readers. My intention is to reveal some of the contradictions that arise from the cultural construction of the falsehood of race.

I was born of an African father, and a European mother with a Jewish heritage, that she was unaware of. It was my auntie, older sister to my mother, who spoke of the Jewish background, showed socialists who were pacifists, some of whom were imprisoned for their pacifism. During the European World War II (1939 to 1945), my mother was a firefighter.

Her mother, a woman of Spanish ancestry, perhaps Sephardim, escaped from a cruel husband and came to live with my grandfather, who was already married. My grandfather and his wife, who were childless, accepted my grandmother, and my mother's mother had their three children. There were professors, artists, stained glass makers, and bell makers in the family lineage. My grandfather was a member of the rail workers' union and had two union medallions with "Workers of the World Unite" enameled on them and my mother gave them to me, one I buried with her and one I still proudly own. My mother was raised by her mother along with the wife of her father. She called them both her mother. Her own mother passed away young, and this was a great sadness to my mother and auntie, who remembered her as a "lovely woman" who was gentle and kind. Although I never met my grandmother, my mother inherited her gentility and generosity. My mother's other mother, whom she remembered well, was good to her and her older sister. She was a seamstress and made the school uniforms and children's clothes they needed. I can remember meeting my grandfather, who was strict and wise.

My father's mother was from the family of Ankrah of the Ga nation. He loved his mother dearly. When he said I looked like his mother, that was such a tremendous honor. He still had half of a photograph of her in a special book that he kept in the bedroom closet on a high shelf; tears welled in his eyes whenever he showed me her image because he had lost the other half of her picture. She was a queen mother, and like my European grandmother, passed away young. It has been told by my family that the Ga people traveled from Sudan 2000 years ago and settled on the coast of West Africa, in a place that European enslavers and colonizers had named the Gold Coast, in 1879, some 5 years before the Berlin Conference and the agreement to divide Africa among Europeans. Sudan meaning land of Blacks or land of slaves[1] did not exist at the time of the Ga migration, but it was called Kush or Nubia and even further back Ta Seti. Above the Sahara, Africa were colonized by the Arabians who brought enslavement down to the West coast. It was not until 1957 on becoming independent from Britain that the Prime Minister, Kwame

---

[1]Explained by the Kushite/Nuba linguist, Tanutamon Gerais at MKA Institute lecture meetings.

Nkrumah, renamed the Gold Coast, Ghana, after ancient Ghana that existed in the areas of today's Senegal, Gambia, and Mali.

My father was raised as a prince by his mother's family (a priest of the Ga spiritual tradition). He told me that this status had no meaning when the British arrived. He was taken away from his mother by his father when he was very young, to be schooled in Freetown, Sierra Leone, to go to university in the UK and become a professional person. My father's father was from Freetown Sierra Leone. He was a Krio descendant.[2] My grandfather was a lawyer.

I spent my formative years in Ghana and Nigeria and learned to speak Igbo and Yoruba when my parents lived in Nigeria. My aunties, uncles, and cousins in London, who descended from Sierra Leone and Ghana, spoke neither of these languages. They spoke Krio and Ga when they were not speaking English, so English became my language of communication. Much like English, Krio, Ebonics, and languages from the Caribbean combined many languages to form a language that all could understand. In many cases, these essentially African languages have European languages incorporated. Ironically, and linguistically, all languages trace back to Africa, which is logical as humanity was born in Africa. Kemet developed the earliest writing that we know of, the Mdw Ntr, although early rock paintings show that writing began even earlier.

As a young woman growing up in the UK, after leaving Nigeria, I rarely met African people in the streets of London, or in my schools, outside of my relatives. However, I met aunties, uncles, and cousins traveling backward and forward from Africa. This was very exciting for my brothers

---

[2]The Krio comprise African Americans, Jamaicans, some of whom were the Black Loyalists who fought for King George III during the American Revolution to win their freedom. One may surmise that his marriage to the Black Queen Charlotte had an impact on George's decision to free enslaved Africans. Conscious that the harvesting of sugar cane was highly profitable and deadly with a life expectancy of 7 years, Charlotte forbade her royal household from eating sugar. Included in the Krio were Jamaican maroons, and liberated Africans. Those who became Krio arrived between 1787 and 1885. As many as 1,200 Black Loyalists may have sailed to Sierra Leone, their descendants as well as those Africans who traveled from Britain, built Freetown.

and me. Many of our relatives were the colonized Africans who had come to Britain to qualify as doctors, lawyers, politicians, journalists, etc., to return to Africa to help build European infrastructure, institutions so necessary for European nation states, to uphold their exploitative reasons for being in Africa. These reasons were related to enslavement, gold, raw materials, and knowledge. Every now and again, I would see someone looking like me and we would wave and acknowledge each other like belonging to a secret society of people who after "darkie," "blackie," and "nig nog" were later termed as half castes and even later, as biracial and possibly bicultural.

Living in London among racists, my whole family suffered the indignities of slurs and threats and altercations. As the eldest child, although I was a girl and we lived under the auspices of race and patriarchy, I had to protect by fighting for my brothers who were vulnerable to assaults as boys from boys. Interestingly, I was not considered a girl at most times, so I think it would have seemed quite comical to see a light skin girl in a school uniform or dress fist fighting with young European male aggressors. More recently, when reflecting on our past experiences of growing up in London, the eldest of my brothers thanked me for being strong, defiant, and a protector. When I wanted to have an African name change ceremony, my father chose Nah, a Ga name, which means protector in both the ancient Egyptian language, written in the Mdw Ntr (hieroglyphics) and is a respected status like Nana in Ghana. There is a question about names that were given to us by enslavers and colonizers that were handed down so that one gives respect to those who, even with Arabic and European names, fought and died in the name of justice and who bore us. Even if our ancestors did not fight, they survived, gave birth, and here we are. The names bestowed upon us were not always who we really were or are; ultimately, it is how we live in the world that we shall be known for.

I went through schooling to learn who I was not. My mother was not a slut or prostitute; my father was not an ape or subhuman; and my brothers and I were not the devil's spawn, born of sin out of the forbidden, immoral liaison between the white and Black races. I always thought of myself as African. What else could I think? The contradiction of being in a racist country that did not even think I was human was a strange dilemma. By the rules of the falsehood of race, I was made less human by my African father and, as it has transpired over time, I am less human today because of my European mother. In both scenarios, I am a betrayer of my so-called race, whichever it may be thought to be, and am potentially trusted by neither. Proving my worth to African people and showing allegiance has been, since young, at the root of my behavior. I have been through processes as I have always had to prove that I am human and put up with open animosity most of my life. I was ashamed to affiliate myself to the whites of Europe with the light skin, who showed their dislike and hatred of me throughout my life in the UK, but I could never ignore the role of my mother in my life. I had to get away from the shame of being light-skinned.

My dear friend, Howard Johnson, born in Jamaica and raised in the United States, a documentary filmmaker who made films on Marcus Garvey, the roots of reggae, Black Hollywood, and many more, told me that logically I could not betray my own mother who breastfed me. I realized I had to find a theoretical location outside of the race paradigm that would enable me to be a proud Black woman with a white mother and a Black father. My belief in myself as a Black woman living in white supremacist beliefs was in part owed to her. She saw the contradictions before I was born and warned me of the world that I had entered, although much of it I could see; she was a guiding light. She helped me know that there were others like her who did not believe in practicing or supporting racism and the racialization of humanity. The Quakers were at one time such a group. One must always be conscious that in the race paradigm, being white, biracial or light-skinned privileges one, and one must use that privilege for the good, like changing the social order.

My father was my mentor. He taught me some of the contradictions of the race paradigm in Africa and Europe, and he did not differentiate my status as an older child and a girl. I had responsibilities and, as a girl, was equal to my brothers. After all, I came from a line of prominent African women. My mother was a brave woman. She always defended and loved her African husband and Black children even when she was an elder and we ourselves were coming toward elderhood. I know that she would have died for us, perhaps she nearly did.

I read about the difficulties of race and the white mother from another vantage point, that of Professor James McBride, who was the chairperson of the newly developed African and African American Studies department at Penn State. Professor McBride hired me to work there when the department first began, and I was most honored. His book, *The Color of Water: A Black Man's Tribute to His White Mother*, speaks of some of the contradictions that he tried to understand growing up in a Black community. His mother, a Jewish woman, grew up among Black people in the South and married two great Black men, fathers, who both sadly passed, leaving her with 12 children to raise. His book speaks of the situation of being a Black man and being raised among 11 siblings in a Black neighborhood enforced by police brutality and social disadvantages. His mother's Jewish heritage, which she rejected, and in many ways, it rejected her because she married into an African/Black family played an important role in her life. Professor McBride felt he could not ignore that heritage and that it was a part of him, as was his mother.

In contradiction to this experience, after my formative awakening in Africa, I grew up in Britain in white communities and was often the only Black/African child at the schools I attended and fought often in the playgrounds and in the streets to stay alive. My mother did not know that she was Jewish, very likely her family tried to protect her as Jewish people were being killed by white supremacists in Europe, while they were also busy killing African people around the world. My mother and Professor McBride's mother had difficulties being accepted; however, in both cases, it was African people whom they felt more accepted by. My mother had few friends, her friends were mainly her children, and our friends became her friends. There were very few white people that she was comfortable with. Most of her friends had Black children who were African or African-Caribbean. Professor McBride (2006) said philosophically, as he grew an awareness of himself during his research regarding his mother's family and ultimately the search for self:

> My own humanity was awakened … There's such a difference between being dead and alive, I told myself, and the greatest gift anyone can give anyone else is life. And the greatest sin a person can do to another is to take away that life. Next to that, all the rules and religions in the world

are secondary; mere words and beliefs that people choose to believe, kill, and hate by. My life won't be lived that way, and neither, I hope, will my children's. (p. 229)

I was raised with African highlife, jazz, blues, bluebeat, ska, U.S. pop like Little Eva, and Tamla Motown, and so on. Throughout my life, I met beautiful people who were Black and white. In the 1960s, young white people were trying not to be white. They were trying to discover themselves, particularly through Black/African music and the arts. I stayed rooted in my Africanness with my African experience, music, the arts, beliefs, growing up, mothering, politics, philosophies, schooling, education, sports, spirituality, healing, love of the mysteries of life and its beauty, love for animals and nature in its myriad forms. As a child, I realized from at least 9 years old that I was here for a reason and that reason was to show that race was a falsehood and that racism was abhorrent, disgusting, despicable, and demonic. I came to know that the treatment of African/Black people, the reprehensible crimes committed against Black humanity, particularly those of the darker hue, like my father, was a murderous fantasy created in the minds of insane people across the world. My father helped me to become conscious by teaching me this reality. He always asked me, "What is truth?" Like so many, I became a truth-seeker. From childhood, I wondered what kind of people would commit such abhorrent crimes against humanity? Continuing along these lines of thought and through my university research and investigation, I learned from great African thinkers, as noted in my bibliographies, that this insanity is locked into the doctrine of white supremacy, a central theme in European culture and practiced by many phenotypes whether privileged or demonized by this belief.

White supremacy is a dogma, a centralized belief, a cult. I have found that it is possible for Europeans, and all other phenotypes imbued with European culture, to not believe or practice this falsehood. Some Europeans actively seek cultural beliefs that oppose these thoughts. They are a silenced voice that can be found among the poor and the rich. That does not mean that by the lack of melanin that they have not been privileged, whether they wanted it or not. They understand that those elites of Europe, the main perpetrators of racism, have debased, dominated, and committed monstrous crimes against their own populations for centuries.

They have impoverished, made homeless, underpaid workers, provided no work, created unemployed collectives, and the unemployable, mistreated violently the mentally, and physically vulnerable, withheld help to the less fortunate and purposely abused, demonized and inferiorized these families inclusive of the mothers, women, and children, and so on. Sadly, people who have historically suffered so dreadfully can still be convinced to practice the doctrine, possibly through ignorance of the truth, or possibly to feel good about themselves, or raise their own status in the social hierarchy and/or prove their allegiance to their elite, so they can profit and/or not be killed.

As African people from the continent and the Caribbean arrived in London as invitees to work, so the terrain changed. Over time, the children who arrived, and those born in London lost their African cultural values and in a generation of growing up in negativity and trying to survive, we infused and assimilated the habits and ways of the mistreated abused European poor. Families with African children were no longer practicing disciplined behaviors, respecting their elders, caring for each other, remembering their ancestors, we began using anti-African/Black rhetoric as weapons of debasement among ourselves. Even wealthier Black/African families lived in poor neighborhoods and were affected. I have taught my own children, to the best of my ability, to be culturally African.

My friends, Carmel Cameron, John Oke, and I started a Saturday school (supplementary school). John created the Camden Black Parents and Teachers Organization; and together, as parents and teachers, we organized conferences on the "education" of the Black child, helped children of differing ethnicities and phenotypes who were being purposely failed in schools; initiated Black organizations; I earned my three degrees investigating the so-called education of Black pupils culturally, politically and philosophically; visited schools around the United States as a voted member of the Council of Independent Black Institutions, CIBI; developed lessons for Black students; traveled to Africa, visiting rural schools; became a published author writing *Afrikan Mothers: Bearers of Culture, Makers of Social Change; The Afrocentric School [a blueprint]* relating to child and curriculum development as well as co-authored a book with Molefi Kete Asante, *Being Human Being, Transforming the Race Discourse.*

I am currently a professor in the Department of Africology at Temple University and have great pride in being an African womanist, promoting African womanism as Afrocentric theory grounded in the ancient principles of Africa before conquest when women, particularly as mothers, were revered and respected Africa-wide as evidenced in Kemet (Ancient Egypt; Dove, 1998a). Moreover, before patriarchy and the debasement of the mother, one can say that the position of the mother in society is evidence of how civilized or uncivilized it is. It has always been my belief that one can take the African model of the past and use it as a model for the future. I am always learning and growing.[3]

Today, the identity of "mixed race" is no longer relevant to some, it is still ensconced in the university setting, even in my own department. Those of the darkest hue across the world remain vulnerable to abuse and mistreatment, governmentally, religiously, politically, philosophically, health-wise, militarily, etc. One can align oneself culturally with one's ancestors. This model offers the logic for a culturally oriented, educative foundation for those who are teachers and learners.

To begin with, we as teachers and learners and those whom we teach should be able to understand three important questions posed by the Afrocentric educationist and psychologist Asa G. Hilliard III[4]:

- Who am I?
- Where am I?
- How on earth did I get here?

---

[3]Sankofa is an Asante Divinity of History and relates to taking the precious important knowledge of the past to build the future. Sankofa is not evolutionist as there is an understanding that ancient ways can be more advanced than current times or possible futures.

[4]Asa Hilliard III was a respected psychologist and educationist, Kemetologist (Egyptologist). He taught teachers and advocated Afrocentric schools that promoted the cultural values of Africa. He wrote *The Maroon Within Us: Selected Essays on African American Community Socialization*. The Maroons were enslaved Africans who freed themselves and over time freed others creating safe spaces to live and practice African ways, the most famous of which is Palmares, an African republic built in the 1600s in Brazil.

The battle for a new future is the battle for the mind. As earlier propounded, it is the mind that guides our thoughts toward eventualities shaped by the realities of culture and living. Culture is shaped by the mind, which in turn shapes culture. This Afrocentric guide is grounded in the belief that by applying truth to cultural history, we have the potential to create the building blocks today for becoming conscious or becoming enlightened. Our hope is that in time, we can imagine and thus manifest a better future than the one many of our children experience and foresee. It is a process.

CHAPTER 11

Some Historical and Cultural Elements

Africa, before conquest, offered a valuable source of knowledge, much of which was purposely hidden and has still to be uncovered. Over 4,500 years ago, an ancient African sage, Ptahhotep, said in his book of wise instruction:

> Be not arrogant because of your knowledge. Take counsel with the ignorant as well as with the wise. For the limits of knowledge in any field have never been set and no one has ever reached them. Wisdom is rarer than emeralds and yet is found among the women who gather at the grindstones. (Karenga, 1984, p. 41)

These words of wisdom, although thousands of years old, reflect written evidence of African ethics that existed thousands of years earlier. The images of Djehuti and Seshat represent the idea of knowledge—truth. They are complements of each other. Often, we see only Djehuti the masculine divinity, but Seshat the feminine divinity is equally important.

Below are the images of the Divine Seshat and Djehuti who are both wisdom keepers or knowledge bearers. Seshat is linked to the building of sacred places like libraries within which sacred knowledge–truth is held. She also carries a seven-pointed star on her head and wears a leopard skin on her body. Djehuti sits upon Maat's scales of justice sometimes as a baboon balance and is also the recorder of a human's life lived, and is considered lord of sacred words, represented with the Ibis head.

The codification of ideas, that is, reflects a system of laws based on beliefs, values, rules, etc. The writing or symbolism reflecting codification happens years after the knowledge, theory, information has been put into action and is known to work. For instance, the movement of the sun, planets, and moon took thousands of years to learn, and ancient knowledge of the pattern in the cosmos was understood years before we find written or symbolic replication that we use for today's calendar although one of the oldest megalithic sites that we know of is in South Africa at Mpumalanga at a place called Inzalo yelanga a Zulu name for the *birthplace of the sun*. It covers thousands of square miles and is possibly 200,000 years old (see air-view pictures of the stones in the photograph below). These stones are astronomically aligned to the planets and are the oldest known calendar.

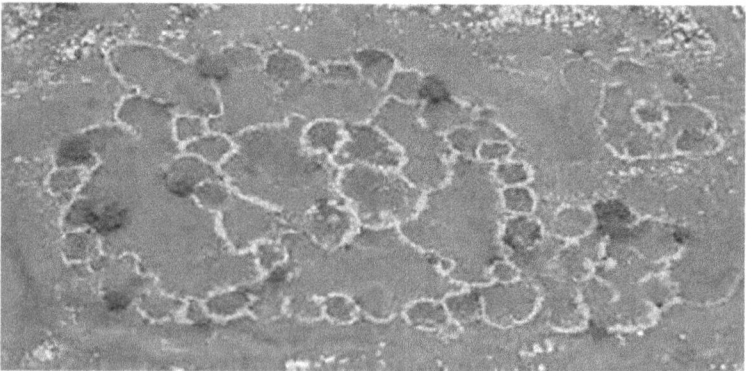

Other evidence is found in the 45,000-year-old Lebombo bone of the Khoisan people of South Africa that provided evidence of the science of astronomy, which dated the movements of the sun and moon in reference to the menses of Khoisan women. The Ishango bone, 25,000 years old, is also a record of the movements of the moon. You will find pictures of and information about the Ishango bone on pages 236–237 in the book *The Afrocentric School [a blueprint]* (Dove, 2021). There is also the example of the Semliki harpoon tip created 90,000 years ago in Congo, showing that modern tools arose in Africa, thereby challenging ideas of backwardness and evolution (Yellen et al., 1995). The wisdom of people like Ptahhotep is written; so in a Eurocentric way, we can understand its truth through African Kemetic knowledge. However, it is important to realize that such wise sayings are linked to an ancient cultural orientation that is morally grounded. We have the ancient principles of Maat, also codified which attest to that reality.

Wisdom ideas have many names, not only in Africa but also across the world through those Africans who left Africa millennia ago and populated the world. Maat in this work is an ancient African set of values and beliefs to aid in living one's life in Truth, Justice, Reciprocity, Righteousness, Harmony, Balance, and Order (Karenga, 2006). Maat was codified in Kemet (ancient Egypt), classical Africa, before the invasions and conquests took place. The laws or ideals of Maat, such as the 42 admonitions or declarations of innocence are used to guide practices and behaviors in modern religions such as the 10 commandments in Christianity and rules of practices in the modern religions like Brahminism, Judaism, and Islam. Ideas of doing good and being righteous appear in other holy texts but culture not only develops ideas but also decides how they will manifest and be viewed and expressed in society. Maat is represented as a feminine divinity with wings. She reflects that there exists order in the enormity of the universe impacting even on individual behaviors and beliefs. Without Maat, there is chaos. It is the responsibility of humanity to seek and enact Maat.

Colonizers and enslavers purposely forbade African cultural beliefs, the mainstay of survival for humanity, under the threat of death for countless people as aggressive cultures corrupted and erased traditional beliefs. The process of historical and cultural erasure in memory and through institutional destruction and name changing became a critical part of conquest and domination. Eventually, the knowledge of the people was forgotten, and the descendants may never know. Colonization, inclusive of replacing indigenous institutions like family, religion, education, economy, governance, politics, science, health care, entertainment, continues to set the stages for maligning the character of Africa and her people by creating a false history of humanity in which the controllers become the original culture makers of "civilizations."

The resulting condition of being alienated from one's own cultural history and, therefore, identity is known as dislocation. This condition happens when the conquered are no longer able to remember their historical and cultural legacy. This is the case for many people in the United States regarding the First Nations people, the original Africans who left Africa thousands of years ago, and the Africans captured and enslaved and brought to the Americas to build the United States for their conquerors. The ability to be free to expand upon cultural remnants is highly prized by many and has been enacted for centuries, and some people do not wish to be found. Maroon societies exist all over the world, the most famous of which was founded in Brazil called Palmares. For more information there, some of the liberationists are named in the book *The Afrocentric School [a blueprint]* in lesson plans for 7 to 8 years.

Africology as an academic discipline strives to provide knowledge grounded in the Black/African experience from ancient to current times. Afrocentricity, the theory that underpins the discipline of Africology, created by Molefi Kete Asante arose from the historical reality of the murderous emancipation struggles of Black people from enslavement, inclusive of the Black students' movement, to create Black studies as an academic discipline in universities across the United States. The current political situation in Florida, led by Governor Ron Desantis, highlights the continuing attempts, through "law," to prevent "education" based on true history, from being told. The current president has empowered these proposed laws, claiming that those who have a true understanding of the cultural historical reality are a danger to U.S. society although they represent the silenced voices of the oppressed. The false history established in relation to the racist "enlightenment" philosophies and the promotion of white supremacy is the one preferred and promoted. Considering Desantis's position, does he know what happened to the First Nations people of Florida before African enslavement? The condition of knowing or coming to know is referred to as "woke" and used as a political fear concept as part of a campaign to ban books and prevent knowledge—truth development as a warning to those who dare to seek truth.

Reconnecting to the cultural historical past has been an impetus for creating the Afrocentric Model of knowledge for teachers and learners of whom we are all. What we learn affects society, and all the institutions of that society whether to reinforce the institutions or dismantle them are choices that we can make based on ignorance or knowledge. Afrocentricity enables us to place Africa in the center of the story of humanity so that we may locate or relocate ourselves and embed ourselves in our own truth. The truth is that, wherever and whoever we are, our ancestors were African and phenotypically deeply melaninated and every person who lives can be connected through mitochondrial DNA to one Black African mother.

The idea that Afrocentric theory can be used by non-African/Black people is a conundrum for Black nationalists and White nationalists if one uses the belief that humanity is divided into races. Afrocentric metatheory has risen out of the construction of race and racism, as a necessary antidote. It is impossible for the African person, the mother and those of the darkest hue, to come to terms with the historically justified murderous treatment of Black Africans and the diaspora for myriad reasons, all over the world (Dove, 1998b). The wicked crimes committed as a necessity, because some people have more melanin than others, are not logical to any clear-thinking human being. Through the illogicity of race, when African/Black people arise to challenge human rights violations, these liberationist acts are viewed as Black or African dilemmas. There is a moral order that remains among phenotypes of differing melanin content in the skin. Maat is more easily understood among the darkest skin people as the illogicity that Black means inferiority even in the so-called Holy texts, helps one to remember or try to remember.

It is an urgent requirement to remember a historical past when race did not exist. Only the more ancient societies can remember this, like the First Nations people of Australia, they are neither racist nor patriarchal. The prevention of knowing one's ancestral location has helped to make the cultural domination more real as without ancestral knowledge, which has been demonized and forbidden, it is almost impossible to know who we are. Other so-called races, phenotypes who have not undergone some of the vileness of abuse meted out to persons of the darkest hue have been privileged to some extent and do not feel compelled or responsible to join in these righteous demands. Because of the years of imposed racist propaganda, they are unable to understand that human rights are inclusive of all humans, and the reality is that we are all human, and all descended from Africa.

CHAPTER 12

Cultural Similarities and Distinctions Among Humanity

Africology has arisen to correct such wrongs through evidence and logic to provide new ways of thinking. The principles espoused by Africology are based on ancient beliefs. Ironically, the principles of Maat, although thousands of years old, are principles that we seek to align ourselves with as a futuristic vision. We have not yet reached our "ancient future" a term used by Wayne Chandler (1999) from his wonderful book of the same name. Afrocentricity is without limit. It has been debased by those who fear its limitless potential. Already, there are Africologists who are Russian, Dutch, Chinese, Bangladeshi, Japanese, Portuguese, Brazilian, and so on, who teach Afrocentricity in their own countries. The late and loved Ana Monteiro-Ferreira (2014) was a Portuguese Africologist, considered white, who employed the theory to critique European constructions of knowledge foundational to inhuman practices. She wrote that:

> Unlike the universal character reclaimed by Eurocentric ideologies, Afrocentricity unapologetically honors historical cultural contingency. This sense of contingency and respect is precisely that which generates the whole encompassing scope of the theory that can be appropriated by anyone anywhere … a liberating theory from any form of oppression, distortions, and dislocation … One does not need to be African to embrace the Afrocentric paradigm as his or her (or their) intellectual orientation in the same way that one cannot assume to be Afrocentric just by being of African descent … Afrocentricity promotes human equality overcoming any socially constructed hierarchies. (p. 167)

Afrocentricity offers a grounded discourse regarding human possibilities, thus, *Teaching Teachers: The Afrocentric Model of Education, The*

Afrocentric School [a blueprint] (Dove, 2021), rejects the race paradigm and gendered hierarchies but explains their synchronistic connection. It offers an authentic Afrocentric guide based on the ancient ideas of the indigenous First Nations people of the world. They were the first Africans to populate the world during the migrations out of Africa, and who viewed earth as a living organism, tied to a cosmos—the sun, moon, stars, planets, environmental experiences that we learn to live in and work with along with the myriad features of nature and life that we are an integral part of. In some sense, the idea of the two-cradle theory explains the differences in thoughts and behaviors so cogently. An aim is to connect these ways of thinking to humans who inevitably can make choices, noting that there is a valid intersection between these cultural orientations that can be considered zones of confluence, which will be explained in light of choices available and made.

Some of us are destroying the planet and living entities in the pursuance of profit by any means necessary. All of us are deeply affected by emissions and outcomes in these decisions. While we are fractured in thoughts, relating to the status of our humanity, regarding these events, of which many of us are unaware, there is very little collective support one way or the other. For example, in Niger in Africa, France is currently negotiating the mining of uranium as a source of nuclear energy that is used to provide electricity. According to the world nuclear association, the French are almost nuclear efficient regarding the source of their electrical power, which is 70% nuclear. The French are also aware that the First Nations people in Canada have campaigned against the mining of uranium since 1930, experiencing the pollution of their lands, nature, water, and the radioactive effects on human biology.

I have lived in Canada and visited some of the polluted lands and have seen the devastation (e.g., lakes with no fish, trees with no birds). Others of us are trying to respect ancient indigenous traditions that have a long history of caring for the planet, who at the same time built amazing civilizations that respected humans, nature, and the environments. The First Nations original people of Australia and their friends are campaigning and marching against the pollution of their lands, lives, nature, etc., by the many large corporations embedded there, like Rio Tinto, BHP, Fortescue Metals, Newcrest Mining, South32, and Evolution Mining.

The false divisions among us prevent us from identifying the companies and their international owners that disrespect and ignore the ancient guardians of the land, the "keepers of wisdom" whose lives are most affected. As a result of our dislocation from each other, each country is segregated from knowledge of the global companies that enter them in search for resources that can be used in the interests of the colonizers or conquerors. The colonizers have never stopped working on colonizing. Race is used as the basis of their decisions. "Whites" or "Arabs" know best, and this can be proven by their wealth and scientific advances. While the countries they control are being bled and the mineral wealth continues to be taken to their own countries. They are totally aware that the mind is the key site for colonization and land control. The repositories of cultural beliefs are firmly instituted in governments and "educational" institutions that successfully school the minds of the colonized. For example, the burning of the rainforests in Brazil and the removal of the myriad forms of life in the rainforests ranging from humans indigenous to these beautiful lands, to plants that are medicinal. It is hoped that the race paradigm that inferiorizes or makes superior or inferior our humanity largely based on skin color and contrived histories can be dismantled. We may view ourselves in more humane ways and discover efficient ancient models that produced natural energy without killing the world.[1] Moreover, it has been shown by scientists that the pyramid itself could produce electrical energy from the sun and the water beneath. The pyramid was covered with casings of limestone reflecting the skies and storing energy within, before the Arabs arrived and took the stones to build their mosques.

This simple guide is an attempt to identify and seek similitude among humans to bring humans together as a continuing part of an ancient human project that is to ultimately live in Maat. In other words, the human objective of higher learning is to become conscious of who we are, why we are here, and how we may live with respect to the environment, nature, and with humanity (Asante & Dove, 2021). In this way, we may live to our highest ideals and become human, which our ancient African ancestors believed is, in its highest form, divine.

---

[1]Further interest in Kemet and the sciences of the pyramids, which still cannot be built today, can be found at https://www.youtube.com/watch?v=ZCkQqNI6EyQ

The pursuance of being human in relation to the principles of Maat, which embodies the idea that there are cosmic laws and human understandings of purpose that we have already understood in the ancient past: Maaticity. Difference, particularly in appearance, is not viewed as problematic in this work. The Afrocentric idea celebrates difference and seeks similitude among humanity. This guidebook aspires to highlight the ancient belief that we, as educators, teachers and learners and in particular seekers of truth, have an important mission. The ancients believed that knowledge was/is the key to enlightenment, and as educators, our role is, as truth-seekers, to find, build upon and teach, the knowledge that can lead us to improving circumstances, the human condition, and living harmoniously.

Molefi Kete Asante is a philosopher; thus, Afrocentricity is philosophically grounded. Applying the classical African terms of ancient Egypt, known by the African inhabitants as Kemet, the philosopher, is called Seba. Philosophy is a Greek word, and when broken down, "philos" means love, friendship, affection, while "sophia" refers to wisdom and knowledge. The teachings of the early classical African Seba influenced the later Greek philosophers (Asante, 2000). Imhotep (2700 BCE), the African Seba, dealt with questions of space, time, volume, the nature of illness, physical, and mental disease and immortality (Asante, 2000). Ptahhotep (2414 BCE) produced the first written ethical teachings that we know of, regarding aging and believing that life is incumbent on making harmony and peace with nature; Kagemni Sage (2300 BCE) taught that humans should perform good deeds for the sake of goodness rather than personal advantage; and Merikare (1990 BCE) focused on the significance of excellent speech and common sense in communication. The Kemetic word *seba*, wisdom, is the root for *sebait* and *sophia*. The Kemetic *sebait* means wise instruction and closely relates to the Greek word *sophia*. It is a way of looking at meaning and explaining and understanding what you see and why you see it in a particular way. It is a method of critical thinking and can be used to interrogate all disciplines. There are cultural differences between philosophy that the Greeks learned from African Sebait. The influence of culture on philosophy will become clear in this model of defining difference along cultural lines. True justice is Maat, and only exists with Truth, Reciprocity, Righteousness,

Harmony, Balance, and Order. These ancient values are embedded in the development of character and are transmitted through culture. In the book *The Republic*, by Plato, there is a discussion of the case for injustice regarding whether a just person is happier than the unjust.

> Glaucon argues that justice, or morality, is merely a matter of convenience. It is natural for men to pursue their own interests regardless of others; but it would be impossible to run an orderly society on that basis, and the system of morality is arrived at as a compromise. But it is only a compromise and has no other authority, as can be seen easily enough by considering how a man would behave if its sanctions were removed. And a contrast between the perfectly "just" and the perfectly "unjust" man shows conclusively that "injustice" is the more paying proposition. (Lee, 2007, p. 40)

The notion of justice and injustice are social concepts learned from Africa. Reviewed and applied from a Eurocentric cultural orientation, they are compromised and thus corrupted. Justice and injustice appear as interchangeable regarding their use value to a human being (man). This is the case in the United States, and this is clear when the history of the United States is investigated. For the African person, whether descended from the enslaved Africans brought here or descended from the First Nations people who created their sacred ancestral lands here, injustice is a way of life and justice is pursued to make social change in which those unjustly treated can be liberated from the chains of despair and disrespect. The struggle toward this end, or future, by those who identify mostly as Black people in America, has been a democratizing element in the United States, from which all people have benefited. It may be said that this desire for true justice has been remembered and transmitted culturally over centuries.

The sad reality is that the idea of justice and humanity already existed among the ancient people who already populated the land we call the Americas and the United States. It was the humility and respect of the First Nations people to visitors that enabled the unscrupulous strangers to enter safely and perform horrendous deeds under the guise of friendship. It was a clash of cultures, Northern cradle and Southern cradle, indeed. The idea of giving thanks to the First Nations people is reflective of the culture that enabled the visitors to survive so many years ago.

Today, the United States celebrates a time that no longer exists and is rather more considered by the descendants of the welcoming nations of the first inhabitants as the beginning of the First Nations Holocaust. There are holocausts all over the world, and they should all be remembered, not celebrated.

CHAPTER 13
Defining Race and Patriarchy

Afrocentric metatheory promotes the idea that the theory or paradigm of *race, that is, white supremacy*, is a cultural construction that evolved from *patriarchal societies* that had established social hierarchies through domination (Dove, 2018). Evidence of the origins of these patriarchal societies can be traced to people who thousands of years after leaving Africa struggled to survive in difficult climatic conditions causing a change in cultural orientation that viewed the women, the potential mothers, a burden to survival according to Cheikh Anta Diop. This manifestation of power usage can be explained by using Cheikh Anta Diop's (1989) cradle theory. All humans today are *Homo sapiens* who lived in Africa over 350,000 years ago and began leaving Africa over 70,000 years ago (Asante and Dove, 2001; Hilliard et al., 1987). They were Black, children of the sun. Differing physical appearances or pheno-types already existed in Africa owing to differing climatic situations from those who lived in the mountains, by oceans, rivers, streams, lakes and lived on different diets as well as taking care of needs in development, perspectives, and lived experiences. Differing African Black phenotypes migrated out of Africa in waves but changed over thousands of years to accommodate the new environments because of the later migrations.

Tracing cultural antecedents to their roots, Cheikh Anta Diop (1989) found distinctions among humanity related primarily to the arrange-ments of female–male power relations. It is the woman and the man who produce life and culture. There are essentially two cradles of civilization, and they exhibit conflicting cultural orientations. The Southern cradle of civilization is Africa from which humanity arose and developed female–male reciprocity, known as Twinlineal in the research of Oba T'shaka (1995) and Complementary as shown in the work of Victor Okafor

(1991). These egalitarian relations were the cultural foundation of Africa. This is logically the cultural orientation that was developed for over 280,000 years prior to the migration of African people to the further regions of the world. This cultural orientation is known as African Matriarchy (Dove, 2018), and within this matrix arose the potential and existence for equality, justice, love, compassion, care, justice, harmony, honesty, truth, logic, and democracy, which is known as Maat. This African matriarchal cultural orientation underpins this Afrocentric Authentic guide whereby one seeks egalitarian ideals for solutions to all problems. The Afrocentric Model is based on the idea that through knowledge of our ancestral connection to the cultural historical past, a link to our common humanity can be made and developed. Recognition of ancestors is based on the idea that in their lives, they worked to the good of those who bore them. The ancestors laid the groundwork for the future; they should be remembered because they laid the path for us to follow so that we are able to remember who we are. The ancestors who will be remembered are those who tried to improve the world. European American Ancestors who created the "Trail of Tears" and First Nation peoples' holocausts did not improve the United States or anywhere and their contribution to life was death. An objective of Africology is to retrieve the cultural and historical memory of the ancient past through the different forms of knowledge left behind, noting, discerning and confronting chaos (Isfet) but always seeking order (Maat). Truth can help us to heal and seek solutions to current problems created by the chaos, lies, and hypocrisy. To this end, it is possible to assert that Molefi Kete Asante's Afrocentric paradigm has played an important conceptual role in changing the world.

After *Homo sapiens* left Africa and populated the world, confronting new environments and surviving them, the second cradle of civilization, the Northern cradle, began to develop. Cheikh Anta Diop perceived hostile environments as causal to cultural changes that occurred thousands of years after leaving Africa where life-giving sustenance for human development was abundant. It is also possible to relate environmental changes to phenotypical changes. In less bountiful environments pertaining to modern Western and Eastern Europe, the domination of the woman by the man evolved. It is called patriarchy. This relationship is perceived as the first injustice explained and defined in African woman-ism (Dove, 2018, 2025).[1] The woman is not inferior to the man. This hierarchal union is reflected in societal institutions like the family, reli-gion, health care, education, politics, governance, entertainment, the arts that uphold society, nation, and country. Diop theorized, based on evi-dence largely linked to histories of conquest, that patriarchal culture is antithetical to African matriarchal cultures that revere and respect the woman particularly as mother (Dove, 1998b). The domination of the woman is the first hierarchy of injustice (Dove, 2018). Dove (2018) fur-ther theorizes that patriarchy provides the basis for the belief in the hierarchy of humanity, the foundation of the theory of race. The inequal-ities of humanity based on color are realized/revealed in the religious thoughts of Brahminism–Hinduism, Hebraism, Christianity, and Islam Muslim. These religious beliefs influenced the later pseudo-sciences that would arise out of Europe (Dove, 1998a, 2018). Although Europe created the concept and theory of race, Europe failed to prove that there was a genetic and racial superiority of white people and/or a genetic inferiority of Black people. This is because there is only one race and skin color does not provide a basis for intelligence. Europe's cultural construction of race is ensconced in the doctrine of white supremacy. White supremacy has and continues to have a murderous impact on the ability of Black people to live. While race is not real, racism is. All social and cultural hierarchies in the United States find Black/African humanity at their bases. All Black people, wherever they come from, particularly those of the darkest hue, are vulnerable to death, despite physical and mental health, wealth, gen-der, sexuality, age, and so on.

This culture-based education model moves away from Eurocentric anthropology and notions of culture founded on the belief in patriarchy, race, and evolution. Using the intersections of patriarchy and race as guides to cultural reality, the least evolved humans are viewed as Black/African women. Societies that place women in egalitarian roles with men are considered uncivilized and primitive. Racist anthropology does not preclude European anthropologists like Franz Boas and Melville

---

[1]African womanism is an Afrocentric theoretical concept, explained in Dove (2025).

Herskovits from stepping outside of the boundaries of race. Boas rejected the idea that cultures were genetically based, and Herskovits (1990[1941]) believed that African people did not lose their cultural values, and beliefs after they were enslaved and stolen from Africa and brought to the United States. Based on his studies in Africa and the United States, Herskovits realized that the good manners paraded by white Southern plantation owners were learned from the graces that African people showed to each other. At the beginning of his book, Herskovits (1990[1941]) humbly dedicates his book "to the men and women who, in Africa and the New World, have helped me understand their way of life."

The Afrocentric education guide is cognizant that racism is very real and continues to affect Black lives cruelly and murderously and on white lives, through privilege, ignorance, and dysconscious racism, which Joyce King (1991, p. 135) defines as "an uncritical habit of mind (including perceptions, attitudes, assumptions, and beliefs) that justifies inequity and exploitation by accepting the existing order of things as given." In other words, the outcomes of racism are accepted by those privileged by it.

The power of the global race construct continually masks the realities of its illogicity. There are so-called white people who have died in Black struggles in the anti-apartheid movement in South Africa. There are white people who live in Black communities like Brixton, Tottenham, and Harlesden in London; there are those who pass for white but have recent African ancestry and those who do not wish to pass for white; then those who are parents of Black children who live in white and/or Black communities. There are white youth who live in Black areas in the UK and have risen with Black youth to fight against police brutality. Two white men were murdered by a white man in a BLM protest in Kenosha, Wisconsin, over the police shooting (seven times in the back) of a Black man, Jason Blake. Clearly, these murders can be perceived as the killing of betrayers of white supremacy or the so-called lovers of Black people known as "N-lovers."

The killer was found not guilty just as if these men were Black, a clear warning that if white people join with Black people in the effort to fight for justice or social change, their humanity becomes blackened, Africanized, and endangered. This is not new for white betrayers but is rarely discussed. In this way, these acts of justice by the so-called perpetrators of injustice are viewed as inconsistencies attributed to a few individuals that are not strong enough to challenge the race paradigm, thus are shifted to the margins of human history. It leaves haters of Black and white people with anomalies that cannot be answered by the theory of race, a central belief of white supremacy, a European doctrine that is formulated in evil and hatred and can be practiced by anyone of any phenotype, gender, sexuality, class, ability, age, etc. It is hoped that such deviations may become open to discussion, through the cultural paradigm and not continuously hidden for convenience.

These types of "race" events also highlight the significance of the meaning of white-on-white crime, which has been central to Eurocentric behavior throughout the centuries. The more recent so-called World Wars I and II, the Serbian, Bosnian, Croatian, and the current Russian and Ukrainian wars fit the description. It can be said that this warring behavior is based on the Northern cradle values that promote violence, murder, and hatred as solutions to problems. Race has been a unifying factor for humanity. It has brought white people together in cultural and "racial" unity to concentrate on the annihilation of and dominion over non-white people. It has brought Black people together to fight for survival and liberation from domination. These reasons are not enough to bring people together based on race. It maintains separations among races so that each supposed race believes that its own unique, racial difference is important so much so that physical, mental, spiritual, psychological, economic boundaries are almost impossible to overcome, like supporting others who may also suffer from domination and genocide. Under the guise of the hierarchy of race, we are encouraged to hate or love each other, not based on character but on looks.

Each institution carries the belief in superiority and inferiority, and we live with these beliefs, creating ways of existing that reify these racist ideas, thereby creating a "Pygmalion effect" in that our beliefs and expectations affect our development and the development of others (Rosenthal & Jacobson, 1968, p. 47).[2] These events also show that race does not preclude a person from learning pro-Black or anti-Black values or becoming

---

[2]Rosenthal and Jacobson's psychological study showed that the teachers' expectations of the students had an impact on their performance.

conscious and stepping over the boundaries of race beliefs, psychologically, mentally, physically, and spiritually. This cognitive condition is one of the worst fears of those who wish to maintain the falsehood. The Afrocentric Model of Education is to provide the logic to:

- Show the illogicity of race theory through truth.
- Explain and provide standards of ethical and moral behavior.
- Promote the idea that people and culture are changeable.
- Deconstruct notions of inferiority and superiority that have no basis.
- Enable children to see their beauty and the beauty of others.
- View phenotypical difference as wonderous.
- Teach pupils that education is a lifelong process of learning who we are, where we are, and how we got here.
- Provide knowledge that builds a platform for creating new knowledge.
- Show developing knowledge and becoming wise is the key to imagining a future.
- Focus on the significance of the teachers' responsibility to teaching the pupils.
- Help pupils to develop their skills in the seven liberal arts—grammar, rhetoric, logic, geometry, mathematics, astronomy, and music.
- Understand that education includes all the above.

Most educational books use the concept of race as the philosophical foundation for developing methods of teaching and learning. Race has been at the root of defining humanity in a hierarchy that has essentially, over time, placed European white-skinned or rather, those of less melanin as advanced compared with all the other so-called races. There is no evidence to prove the falsity that, based on the melanin content of the skin, and certain phenotypical features, misidentified as race, any group can be viewed genetically, superior, or inferior to another.

Central to the Afrocentric Model of Education is the knowledge that the invention of race is not only socially constructed but is also culturally constructed. The recognition of the racialization of humanity as a cultural condition enables culture to take on a more significant meaning for those educators and pupils whose supposed racial identity has been constructed to be inferior or superior. This serious condition is taken on board and tackled in the Afrocentric Model. Currently, for educators and pupils, race identity is promoted. It follows that if race is not real, then race identity is not real.

What I am suggesting is that the concept of cultural identity is a critical feature of an educational process whereby one can come to know oneself. The scientific reality is that we all descended from our African ancestors. This Afrocentric Model of Education is *not* grounded in the idea that human differences are racial and genetic, but cultural. Cultural distinctions among people become critically important to analyzing past thinking and laying the foundation for future thinking regarding the cognitive development of children and promoting a just world. The model focuses on cultural identities as culturally oriented. How long we may have been dislocated from the first human culture is debatable, and Afrocentric theory allows us to relocate ourselves culturally and historically from ancient times.

CHAPTER 14
Divine Mothers

The Images of Women Divinities as Mothers were very Important to Kemet's Spiritual Life. Het-Her is commonly known by her Greek name, Hathor. She was a very ancient divinity from Kush/Nubia before the dynasties of Kemet. She is associated with healing, love, music, dance, and childbirth and sometimes manifests as the cow who is respected as the epitome of the mother. One can understand how the cow would become sacred in India in her memory as mother. The Hindu or Brahmin religion is associated with the sacred cow who is a manifestation of Het-Her. Interestingly, when investigating the origins of the Brahmin religion, the Black Harrapan people of the Indus Valley Civilization had created a civilization that was built upon African matriarchal beliefs where the women were respected and they people created incredible architectural buildings on the level of Kemet and were literate. When the Indo-Aryans a patriarchal conquering people arrived, early representation of the later types that rule in our current times, they took the lands and controlled the civilization and created a religious racialized hierarchy where they placed themselves at the top as the masters and educators and called it Brahminism after their God Brahma. The Black Harrapan people were called Sudra and placed at the bottom of the religious hierarchy called caste. Those who intermarried produced children who became outcastes and they became "untouchables." The divine cow of Het-Heru is a remnant of the religion of the ancient Harrapan people who practiced African matriarchy in the work of Ivan Van Sertima are known as Kushites.

Auset is commonly known by her Greek name of Isis: She is often depicted feeding her son Heru and is sometimes considered the first Madonna in Christianity, although she is thousands of years older. She had a great following in Europe, East and West. The Notre Dame Cathedral of Paris was built on the top of an ancient sacred site where

A Great Bath at Mohenjo Daro in Pakistan.

There are many sites of the great Indus Valley civilization of the Black Harappan (considered Kushite by Van Sertima researchers). Conquered by the Indo-Aryans who created the Brahmin religion.

she was revered. Auset has also been connected to the Black Madonna heavily revered in the Christian church before becoming white. Auset, famously resurrected her husband Asar, known by his Greek name Osiris, the divinity of nature. Asar was killed by his jealous brother Set, and cut into 14 pieces, Auset gathered those pieces from all over the world, finally finding the last part of his body, the penis, resurrecting her beloved Asar and together they procreated their son Heru. This birth of Heru known in Greek as Horus is sometimes known in Christianity as the virgin birth.

Mut is the Kemetic name for mother. Mut is an ancient divinity from the south and considered the mother and protector of the ruler. She sometimes manifests as the vulture and the lion. Mut is considered the wife of Amun a creator divinity who was powerful in Kush/Nubia and Kemet. Many of the Kandakes were named Amani after their divinity Amon. Importantly, Amun rises out of the nun, with his partner Amunette. Amun is known as the unseen, the Mother and Father of humanity. Sometimes changes occur in the status of divinities, and one may become more popular owing to the needs of the culture and society. It can also be said that conquerors make such distinctions during their rule. Sekhmet is an ancient lion mother divinity and is considered the protector of kings and queens and represents Upper and Lower Egypt. She is associated with Mut, possibly one of Mut's manifestations. She is also viewed as a manifestation of Het-Her. As a divine mother, she is related to healing and medicine.

Neith is considered the mistress of the bow. Ta Seti, land of the bow, is the oldest known Nile Valley civilization that came before Kemet, which may be associated with her name. Neith is a creator, divinity. During her existence, she has been known as a divine mother and affiliated with birth, wisdom, and war.

The cultural and historical role and position of women in society is important to this Afrocentric Education guide. Women are engaged in everything that takes place on every plane of existence. Racism and patriarchy have demoted the Black woman to the lowest position in the hierarchy of humanity, so she has been taken from her rightful place in terms of our reverence for her humanity and the critical role that she has played throughout time as a creator of life and culture. Please locate the picture of the statue of Queen Nanny. Nanny of the Maroons, referred to as Queen Nanny, was a freedom fighter in Jamaica. She fought in the first maroon war against the British in 1720 to 1739. Queen Nanny (see below), stands in Moore Town, Jamaica, following in the footsteps of the Kandakes of Kush, led her people from enslavement and built a town in the Blue Mountains of Jamaica. She was an Akan from Ghana.

Harriett Tubman was born between 1820 and 1822. She was the greatest African warrior in North America during enslavement. See statue below from Peekskill, New York.

Harriett Tubman freed a thousand enslaved African people on her own life saving missions with the underground railroad and with the Union Army in the civil war. Harriett Tubman embodied the fearless spirit, legacy, and memory of Kandake Amanirenas, of Kush. It can be said considering what is proposed here that the culture of her African matriarchy was transmitted to her in her dreams, which she experienced throughout her journeys that guided her to follow her intuition and to use the stars as her guide.

FEMINISM AS RACIST THEORY

The modern recognition of patriarchy by feminists is not linked to a cultural history of humanity linked to Africa. Feminist theories are not aware that there was a different relationship between women and men before patriarchy. This is in line with European academia, which is both patriarchal and racist. Feminists often consider patriarchy to have been the foundation of civilization as they follow classical academic European history. This idea is based on the European anthropological notion of patriarchy, that patriarchy, a feature in human evolution, was formed at the beginning of civilization. However, patriarchy took place thousands of years after African matriarchy. It has been established that African matriarchy was foundational to reciprocity in women's and men's power relationships. Both were respected, as were all genders. Feminist theory puts the blame on the man, and as a consequence, women and men become detached in the struggle rather like the structure of race and the condition of racism. We become segregated and separated and dislocated. The culture that creates this dislocation is the problem. The culture of African matriarchy is the solution, and the blame is with the culture. African matriarchy espouses the complementarity of the woman and the man, the mother and the father of humanity. It is the culture that we hope to teach and imbue to create a more egalitarian society. Maaticity is the route to becoming human. Maat is the foundation of African matriarchy.

Gender is explained in the Philosophy of Djehuti. The Djehuti writings of wisdom are called by the Greeks, Hermetic Principles. Below, Djehuti is seen as the Ibis-headed divinity. He is seen in the "weighing of the heart" as the Ibis-headed divinity writing the record of the deceased life. He is also portrayed as a baboon sitting on the scales of justice in the process of the "Weighing of the Heart." He is sometimes accompanied by Seshat, his female counterpart. You may find these images in the photographs provided.

Djehuti is the transmitter of wisdom through thought and writing and represents the embodiment of scientific and literary accomplishments.

- Gender exists in everything; everything has its masculine and feminine principles.
- Gender manifests on all plains, the physical, the mental and the spiritual.
- On the physical plane, gender manifests as sex.
- Gender is the foundation of creation.
- Life cannot exist without the principles of gender.
- Feminine and masculine are not considered opposites; they are two shades of gender.
- All humans embody all shades of gender.
- Gender can be viewed on a scale represented by a pole, with female and male at either end.
- Those psychologically and physically closer to the female end are called women, and those closer to the male end are called men.
- The gender pole recognizes more than two types of sex (Kybalion).
- Gender roles are defined by cultural beliefs and values. Before conquest, these roles had equal value in Africa (Chandler, 1999).

Please go to the photographs to see the picture of a painting from the 12th dynasty that depicts a tomb procession of a person called Djehutyhotep who is entering the afterlife as an ancestor who is going to meet his divinity Djehuti. The ritual involved in becoming an ancestor is clearly shown with respect and possibly with music and celebration for a life lived well. One can understand the cultural continuity of the belief in striving to become ancestors by living good lives.

The Afrocentric teacher, using my model, must look at history with respect to the voices of those who have been removed from the human history in which we are all participants. The model lays a foundation for understanding how important it is for children to grow up knowing who they are. The information that they receive should help them to understand what Asa Hilliard III told us that we should know: Who am I? Where am I? How did I get here? We are sadly compromised and even disabled if we cannot answer these three important questions. Currently, there are attempts to limit even what little we know by preventing schools in places like Texas from discussing African American and, thus, American history. Moreover, books that can bring light to these areas of information are being banned. Some of the works of Molefi Kete Asante, whose Afrocentric theory is the foundation of this guidebook, were banned in the state of Florida. In response to the myriads of problems relating to "Education," this model enables the teacher and learner to question the authenticity of race philosophy and theory underpinning terms like cultural plurality, multiethnicity, and mixed-race education.

This guidebook views all people in the world as culturally linked to Africa the mother of humanity. This suggestion is a reality that one may call futuristic although it is based on ancient reality that is still unknown. In proclaiming this cultural link, much research must be and is being done to correct the demonization and debasement of Africa and the

African character. Using race-bound education pedagogy serves to perpetuate negative ideas that justify:

- The wanton killing of Black African people, she, he, and they.
- The ongoing genocide of First Nations, indigenous people of every phenotype situated everywhere in the world.
- The reluctance of African people in the United States to identify with a cultural origin or connection to Africa.
- The inability of members of the so-called "races" to perceive that they have a common human and cultural, ancestral connection.
- The perpetration and perpetuation of hostilities among people based on social hierarchies, accompanied by notions of superiority and inferiority.

The Afrocentric feature of discovery, analysis, and investigation can link all people to their African cultural origin. This new way of thinking and philosophizing enables the teacher and learner to seek the route to relocating, reestablishing, reconnecting to African matriarchal beliefs and values, the foundation of Maatic principles.

CHAPTER 15

Timeline of KMT Chronology of Events and Invasions

Eduard Meyer Berlin Chronology is unsupported by evidence/contradicts evidence, which is officially used by Egyptology. In this way, the origins of Kemet are reduced, to deny its Black African genesis.

Manetho Egyptian Priest (285 BC) commissioned by Ptolemy II Philadelphus to write history of Egypt based on historical data. Manetho's dating is about 2,500 years earlier than Berlin Chronology. Robin Walker's research in *When we Ruled* uses this chronology. Manetho's dates are used when evident.

Pre-Kemet	Inzalo yelanga, considered 200,000 years old, oldest megalithic site that we know of. It is aligned with the stars, called *birthplace of the sun* a Zulu word. Located at Mpumalanga, in South Africa.
5900	Solar calendar operating and Creation Story Ta Seti 5900 Kush/Nubia, North Sudan-South Egypt. Bruce Williams, evidence of Dynastic existence (incense burner) at least 150 years before Narmer/Menes
Egyptology Dates	Manetho's Dates
Dynasty 1–2 3150–2649	Old Kingdom 5717
	Dynasty 1 Narmer/Menes 5660–5598 Palette depicts the conquest of Lower Egypt and the uniting of Upper and Lower Egypt by Narmer/Menes

	Hor-Aha
	Djer 5581–5524
	Queen Regent Neith-Hotep 5581
	Female Pharaoh Mer-Neith 5524–5507

Abydos, burial place even for earlier dynasties known as Dynasty 0 Writing developed.

2880	The book of Ptahhotep

Dynasty 3–6	Old Kingdom
2649–2150	3rd Dynasty 5046–4872 Built Pyramids, wrote Pyramid Texts, used Solar Calendar
	Pyramid Age Transformation—no actual timeline for pyramids-age far more than Egyptology official age
2630	Djoser 5018–4989 builds Pyramid complex city Saqqara
2575	Dashur & Giza Pyramids
2400	King Unas 4435–4402 (Tomb) Pyramid Texts— Genesis of *The Book of Coming Forth by Day*
	6th Dynasty 4402–4188

Pepi I 4355–4302
Female Per aa Nitocris 4200–4188
Queen Neferu, possibly the first to hold the title of Divine Wife of Amun

2396–2356	

Dynasty 7–10	First Intermediate Period 4188–3448
2300–2065	4188–3448
	Coffin Texts, restatement of Pyramid Texts written on coffins. *The Book of Going Forth by Day*

8th Dynasty 4188–4042
9th Dynasty 4042–3633
10th Dynasty 3633–3448

Dynasty 11–12	11th Dynasty 3560–3405
<u>2040–1763</u>	Mentuhotep II 3475–3424
	Unifies KMT—capital Waset/Thebes/Luxor
	Middle Kingdom 3448–3182

Admonitions of Ipuwer (A time of great upheaval) Hyksos from Asia.

"A man regards his son as his enemy ... the tribes of the desert have become Kemites everywhere ... what the ancestors foretold has arrived at fruition ... the land is full of confederates, and a man goes out to plough with his shield ... indeed, hearts are violent, pestilence is everywhere, blood is throughout the land, death is not lacking, and the mummy-clother speaks even before one comes near it. Indeed, the land turns round like a potter's wheel; the robber is a possessor of riches and the rich man has become a plunderer ... barbarians from abroad have come to Kemet. Those who were Kemites have become foreigners and thrust aside ... and the man of rank can no longer be distinguished from him who is nobody ... All is ruined."

The Eloquent Peasant Khun Anup a story that reflects on the changing society and its move away from the ancient values of Maat.

12th Dynasty 3405–3182

1897	Amenemhet 3405–3376 constructed Labyrinth 3,000 apartments
Dynasty 13–17	Second Intermediate Period 3182–1709
1783–1550	Nomadic Semite & Asian invasion 3182
	Per aa Khatire 3008 first known *non-African* Indus Valley Civilization–Harrapan flourished 2895
1770	Birth of Abraham in Asia Ur considered father of the Hebrews (Jews)
	15th Dynasty 2545–1993, 16th Dynasty 1993–1709
1675	Hyksos Semitic conquest 2545–1709 widespread destruction
1670–1675	Abraham & family enter Africa
	17th Dynasty, Queen Aah Hotep held the title of Divine Wife of Amun

Dynasty 18–20	
<u>1550–1170</u>	New Kingdom 1709–1095 Temple & Imperial Age
1575–800	Theban recension
1500–800	Aryan conquest of Indus Valley Harrapan Civilization
1550	Ahmose I 1709–1683 and wife Amose–Nefertari (Mother of Amenhotep I) defeat Hyksos
1473	Hatshepsut *Female* Per aa 1650–1600
1391	Amenhotep III (Memnon) 1538–1501 son of Mutemwia, reigns with Queen Tiye Great Royal Wife
1353	Amenhotep IV/Akhenaten 1501–1474 son of Amenhotep III and queen Tiye Per aa Akhenaten—reigns with Nefertiti (seven daughters) (new capital Armana) Aten is the one God.
1333	Per aa Tutankhaten/Tutankhamun 1480–1468 warrior king son of Akhenaten, grandson of Queen Tiye
1320	Moses born in Africa 19th Dynasty 1450–1236
1306	Seti I 1450–1395 father of Rameses II (Rameses the Great) With Het-Heru after life
1290	Rameses II & Nefertari 1394–1328 (67 years)
1259	Peace Treaty of Kadesh uniting KMT with Hatti made between Rameses II and Hattusili
1230	Rameses III sent voyages to ancient America—linked to Olmec of Mexico
1230	Moses—civil war against Rameses II
1190	Moses disappears (dies?)
Dynasty 21–24 1070–750	3rd Intermediate Period—Decline
940	22nd Dynasty Libyan rule Shoshonq I
814	Phoenicians, mainly Black Africans but not only establish Carthage, the birthplace of Hannibal, the general who crossed the Alps with African

	elephants to fight against Roman conquest in 216 BCE. Carthage is today's Tunisia. Nile Valley Africans lived in Carthage and according to Prof Robin Walker, from Greek sources, the greatest temple in Carthage was the Temple of Imhotep known at that time as Asclepius.
700–500	Pentateuch five books of Moses Holy Torah-Version of *Book of Coming Forth by Day*. Distorted-Corrupted by Hebrews living in KMT (supposedly words of God passed to Moses then passed to Scribes)
Dynasty 25	African Cultural Renaissance Period 785–664 (began during 24th Dynasty)
750–675	Kushite African rule from *Napata*, Kush or Nubia Piye, Piankhi Shabaka Stone attributed to Shabaka Per aa (from possibly, 1st Dynasty or 19th Dynasty) Taharqa
667	Assyrians Semites take Lower KMT
664	Assyrians Semites take Upper KMT
Dynasty 26	
664–525	Saite indigenous Kings from the Delta Saite-recension (allowed restrictions on the Greek entries to be lifted)
450	Herodotus Greek Historian
Dynasty 27	
525–404	Persian Aryan Cambyses (continuation of Greek research = enlightenment) Socrates 469–399 Plato 427–347 Aristotle 384–322
Dynasty 28	
404–399	Persian Aryan expelled

Dynasty 30	
<u>380–343</u>	Last Indigenous Rule
Persian	Locate their roots to Indo-Aryans
343–332	
Greek	European
332–30	
332	Alexandria of Macedonia defeats the Persians and conquers KMT
323	Ptolemy I establishes Ptolemaic Dynasty
285	Ptolemy II commissions Manetho to write History of KMT—only surviving record of Dynastic rulership. Manetho dates KMT to 5717
284–314	The Kandakes of Meroe were the queens of the Kingdom of Kush dating from Ta Seti 5900 BCE who ruled from the city of Meroe located in today's Sudan.
250–100	Septuagint version of Pentateuch first Greek version of Hebrew distortion of *The Book of Coming Forth by Day*, explicated by 72 writers, Rabbis, Scribes, written in Alexandria, by African Hebrews, 45 books "The Alexandrian Canon" used by earliest Greek and Latin Church.
196	Rosetta Stone—Decree to celebrate the kingship of the Ptolemy IV. The Mdw Ntr written on the Rosetta Stone, deciphered by Champollion (& Young), in 1822 using Demotic [Hieratic] and Greek writing on stone.
69–30	Cleopatra VII born and rules to death
Roman	European
<u>30 BCE–323 ACE</u>	Conquest of Egypt (Romans rule North Africa)
30	August Caesar claims Egypt, province of Rome
40–10	Queen Amanirenas the Kandake (Queen) leader entered the occupied territory, attacked towns and destroyed the statues of Caesar. Won the independence of Kush (Meroe, Napata) from Roman conquest.
300	Ancient Ghana flourished (older ruins beneath)

Byzantine	Greek Roman Turkish
323–642 ACE	Constantine first Christian Emperor of Rome convenes the first—Council of Nicea
391	Christian Emperor Theodosius bans ancient religious system orders closing of all Temples
527	Christian Emperor Justinian closes last Temple at Philae
	Christianity rising religion
550	European version of Babylonian Talmud interpretation of 6th century—racist interpretation of Pentateuch by European Rabbis and other scholars. Noah and his three sons Ham Black, Shem Semite, and Japeth Aryan.
642	Conquest of Egypt by Arabians (Semites)
651–Present	Islamic Period Semitic
670	Holy Qur'an compiled based on teachings of Old and New Testaments.
700	Ancient Ghana becomes an Empire
1240	Ancient Ghana ends
1250	Mamelukes conquer Egypt (enslaved soldiers of Islam)
1517	Turks conquer Egypt
1765–1783	American Revolution
1789–1799	French Revolution
1791–1804	Haitian Revolution, the first revolution of enlightenment. The most powerful challenge in these modern times to challenge the race paradigm and bring African matriarchal values into the notion of "democracy."
1798	Napoleon of France conquers Egypt "Egyptology" created.
1881	British Ottoman control Egypt
1822	Champollion and Young, decipher the Rosetta Stone

A LIST OF AFRICAN TERMS

A context for, along with brief explanations and suggestions for how they may relate to educational practice:

1. Maat

- **Definition:** An ancient African ethical system emphasizing seven principles, Truth, Justice, Reciprocity, Righteousness, Harmony, Balance, and Order.

Maat is the oldest set of moral/ethical principles pre-dating modern religions. Maat rose out of and is foundational to cultural beliefs in matriarchal societies in which women and men, the producers of life and culture, are respected equally. Women and men sought the divine in their relationships as they were the producers of life and society. In this process, they developed the seven principles of Maat in their relationships from families to nations and nation states like early Kemet. These principles would become the foundations of ancient societies. These societies believed that one should try to live in Maat so that an order prevailed so that people could live in peace with each other and seek solutions in applying Maat to their everyday lives. Some societies today still practice African matriarchy and Maat. Some people try to live by the principles of Maat. The reverence for the ancestors is based on the knowledge that those qualified to become ancestors are those who lived their lives in Maat, which sought to be kind, loving, compassionate, caring, considerate, and good. Maat is not rigid recognizing that we are not perfect but strive to be better.

> Please refer to pages 181 and 326–327 in the book *The Afrocentric School [a blueprint]*. The 42 Declarations of Innocence of Maat are to state what one has not done to bring disorder into the world, for example, 1. I have not done evil. 2. I have not robbed someone with violence. 3. I have not stolen. According to Anthony Browder (1992) in the book *Nile Valley Contributions to Civilization*, these 42 Declarations of Innocence were written at a conservative estimation, some 1,500 years before the Ten Commandments were written in the Biblical texts.

Maat is considered the ontological unity between the higher power and the human. There is the recognition that there is a metaphysical relationship between humanity and all that exists.

In practice, there should be time set aside during which children form a circle and breathe evenly together, close their eyes and calm down and view themselves as important members of the classroom collectives with a mission to bring these principles into their lives, and into the world. The classroom collective comprises a group brought together who can work together to help each other and do the best that they can do. The environment should be less of a competition among each other and more of a collaboration. The competition is one of a personal nature where one tries to improve. African cultural beliefs uplift the notion of the collective because that is the source of improvement for the individual, who is highly prized by the collective.

Each principle can be defined by the educator, and then, the pupils can describe in their own words the meaning of the principles of Maat and why they are important. In time, they may give examples of how these principles exist. Bringing peace to themselves, the pupils can more easily understand the meaning of these principles and reflect on them giving examples of what they do or might do to live these principles.

Practical ways to integrate Maat into classroom values (e.g., restorative justice practices).

The educator can discuss with pupils how injustices can happen when one does not know truth. One may have been lied to or taught things that are not true. A person may believe that a lie is true. If people believe in things that are not true, they may make bad decisions without realizing. Provide examples of believing that someone stole something but did not. What could happen to the person because of the lie? What reasons could make a person lie and know that she/he/they are not being honest.

Here are some untruths:

The amount of melanin in the skin shows whether a person is intelligent or unintelligent.

The more melanin a person has, the more unintelligent.

The less melanin the person has, the more intelligent.

The amount of melanin in the skin shows whether a person is good or bad.

Women know less than men do.

People who are both women and men are inferior to women and men.

Here are some truths:

There is only one race; it is the human race.

Africa is the birthplace of humans.

The original modern persons were called *Homo sapiens*.

They were born 300–350,000 years ago.

We are all *Homo sapiens*, which means wise humans

Any *Homo sapiens* person of 350,000 years ago looks just like any human today, especially a dark skin person.

The first modern persons were African and Black.

The first civilizations came out of Africa.

The first sciences and schools came out of Africa.

Every human on this earth is descended from Africa and African people (explain).

We are the Diaspora (explain).

Phenotypes are not races.

Phenotypes show differences in skin color, hair textures, eye colors, heights, and so on, because of:

Environmental factors that take place over thousands of years create changes in our physical appearances.

Mothers and fathers with different phenotypical looks produce new phenotypes in their children.

Some of the films that show these prejudices can be viewed by the children like "Ethnic Notions" that look at stereotypes of phenotypes inclusive of First Nations, Japanese, Arab and African, etc., and show false beliefs about who people are based on their looks.

Even though we look different as phenotypes, we are 99.9% the same. We may have a blood transfusion to save our lives, from a human who is a different color and gender.

We need to know *truth*, to make *just* decisions.

The pupils will have to define the meanings of each of the seven principles of Maat: Truth, Justice, Reciprocity, Righteousness, Harmony, Balance and Order. What do they mean? How do these principles work together? Please provide examples of how these principles work. It is important to understand that these principles work with each other. Is it possible to have Justice without Truth?

Create a roundtable discussion of pupils who represent different countries in the United Nations. They may choose countries that are not in the United Nations. Why are not all countries members of the United Nations? The pupils should discuss how to stop poverty or feed the world's children or clean the toxic waste in the streams, rivers, and oceans. What is the truth of the situation? How can we solve the problem? Note that there are borders around each country and within these borders that are different cultural orientations, languages, and religions. There are wars going on. These are questions that must be investigated before the roundtable discussion so that the pupils come to the table with ideas. What did you know before the research? What did you discover? Are there young people's groups in the world who look at these situations? How can you join one or start your own?

This work is called Philosophy and Logic.

2. Kemet

- **Definition:** The ancient name for Egypt, signifying its African origins.

Kemet is located in Africa by the River Nile and is known as the oldest nation state that we are aware of. This is important to know, because the nation states that came after, tried to imitate Kemet. Kemet has been dated as far back as 7,000 to 10,0000 years BCE based on the findings of geologists like Robert Schock who examined the water erosion of the great "Sphynx" called by African people of the time Her Em Akhet meaning Heru of the horizon. Heru is the son of Aset his mother and Asar his father. They are a divine family, the example that Kemetic society tried to live up to. The power of the mother was important to Kemet's society. Aset was the divine-caring mother, and there are statues built to show her love and her power that she used for healing. There are many images of Aset as mother. You may find her representation on page 272 in *The Afrocentric School* feeding her baby Heru and sitting next to her husband Asar. They are a loving family who represent living in Maat. They use the seven principles of Maat to guide them. Aset, the mother became known, thousands of years later, as the Madonna in Roman Catholic Church. She was known as the Black Madonna and later adored as Mary the mother Jesus. Birnbaum (2001) writes about the significance of the mother in her book, *Dark Mother: African Origins and Godmothers*. She traces the "dark mother" reverence back to pre-*Homo sapiens* and is cognizant of the African origin of civilization aligning the African mother to the mother of humanity.

The dating of Kemet is not known exactly. We know that the priest Manetho was commissioned by the Greek Pharoah Ptolemy II, Philadelphus, in 285 BCE to find the ancient timeline of the Per aa. Per aa is the African name for the Greek status of Pharoah. Manetho successfully carried out his research and dated the history of the first Per aa in KMT to 5,717, some 2,500 years older than the starting dating given by the official European school of Egyptology by Eduard Meyer who produced the Berlin Chronology based upon the idea that the calendar of the Egyptians, which we use today, was based in its complexity on the rising of Sirius. There was no evidence to support this idea. It not only contradicts Manetho's findings of 30 dynasties but also the findings of well-known European Egyptologists like Flinders Petrie and Alan Gardiner. While Petrie and Gardiner believe that Kemet was European in origin, Egyptologist Wallace Budge writes in his important work, which translates the sacred writing of the Mdw Ntr, *Egyptian Hieroglyphic Dictionary*, vols. I and II, that linguistically, the Mdw Ntr is African.

The modern calendar of the hours, days, months, and years was created before dynastic Kemet thousands of years ago. We know the San people of South Africa created the Lebombo bone, 45,000 years ago that shows the movements of the moon in relation to the menses of the woman. Mathematics and geometry are evidenced by the structures of the pyramids, which cannot be replicated by the modern tools of today. The right angles are used in modern buildings, see pages 168–172 in the book *The Afrocentric School*. This is why the Greek priest philosopher Pythagoras, born in 580 to 750 BCE and trained in Kemet, was not the father of geometry.

The great pyramids were built during the time known as the old kingdom, which according to Manetho's dates, were between 5660 and 4188 BCE. Pythagoras' teachers taught him that there was an order in the universe that is a manifestation of mathematical relations. In other words, there is an order of planetary arrangements that can be found mathematically. Please refer to *Nile Valley Contributions to Civilization* by Anthony Browder for information on Kemet's scientific achievements. Kemet has the largest collection of buildings, artifacts, graves, jewels, statues, potteries, paintings and written knowledge of the sciences, values, beliefs, philosophies, practices they created, which shows what these ancient African people thought and how they lived. Women at that time had great powers as mothers, they were politicians and leaders, healers, physicians, farmers artisans, medical doctors, mathematicians, and priestesses. There were scientists during the old kingdom, which began in 5660 BCE according to Manetho's dating.

Ta Seti existed prior to Kemet and was considered predynastic until evidence was found that showed royal tombs, and that Ta Seti was dynastic before the first dynasty of Kemet. Qustul at Ta Seti was in Kush and lay 100 miles south of Aswan that has now become dammed and Qustul, and all the artifacts of this Kushite civilization lie beneath the Aswan dam that flooded the area. In this way, the falsehood of the idea that Kush sometimes known as Nubia is an imitation or follower of Kemet remains an Egyptological illusion. The works of Charles S. Finch III a well-known Kemetologist and a medical physician who can read the Mdw Ntr and attest to these findings as have other African scholars like Ivan Van Sertima who use the work of Bruce Williams that confirmed the dynastic Kushite reality. Charles Finch's latest work on *Nile Valley Civilization: A 10,000-Year History*, is an important work providing a chronology of the Nile Valley Civilization.

In Kemet physicians were skilled in treating different ailments, some performed complex surgery that influenced the medical treatments of the Medieval period in Europe. The papyri of medicines are evidence of the skills of these physicians. From earlier work on "Medicine" by Dove, found in the *Encyclopedia of African cultural heritage in North America*, whereby ancient medical healing was linked to African healing that came to North America through enslavement and the First Nations people who practiced it before the arrival of captured African people. Like the ancient treatments, it is to be realized that medicine is also spiritual. Spiritual health was the foundation of traditional African medicine. These ancient papyri show the complexity of African medical skills in Kemet. Note that these papyri are owned by Europeans as Black African antiquities but are rather viewed in the light of Egyptologists. There is also a wealth of these treasures owned in private collections and religious collections in places like the Vatican.

Kahun Papyri,

Ramesseum Papyri,

Edwin Smith Papyrus,

Ebers Papyrus,

Hearst Papyrus,

London Papyrus,

Berlin Papyrus,

Carlsberg Papyri,

Chester Beatty Papyri,

Brooklyn Papyrus.

There were more than 100 prominent women physicians in the old kingdom and Lady Preseshet was the director. Women were revered as mothers and protectors of their families and leaders of the nations. Kemet was essentially matriarchal as can be attested to in the legal rights that they had and their important roles in, society, religion as divine protectors. Each conquest from the Hyksos, Assyrians, Persians, Greeks, Romans as Christians and finally the Arabs with Islam forced patriarchal values into the country. The lamentations or documentation by Ipuwer at the time of great upheaval provides a testament to the nature of the conquest by the Hyksos' violent and bloody conquest who stayed in Kemet from 2545 until 1709 BCE. The Per aa Ahmose and his wife Queen Ahmose Nefertari brought back peace after the expulsion of the Hyksos. Ahmose Nefertari was one of the most remembered and loved Queens for centuries after her passing into ancestorhood. It was in the 25th dynasty in 750 BCE when the Kushites returned and brought in the women leaders to take up powerful positions in KMT that matriarchal values began to reappear and become strong again. These Kushites are the same ones who built Ta Seti, which existed prior to Kemet. They maintained their matriarchal beliefs. Ta Seti was known as land of the bow referring to the ability of the great and remarkable accuracy that the arrow could be fired. It was as much a women's domain as well as men. The divinity of the bow in Ta Seti was Neith who was a divine mother and mistress of the Bow.

For courses on mathematics that represent the Kemetic logic, please refer to the book *The Afrocentric School [a blueprint]*, pp. 234–240.

This work is mathematical.

3. Djehuti

- **Definition:** Known as Thoth in Greek, Djehuti is the ancient African divinity of wisdom, knowledge, and writing.

Djehuti is a divinity in Kemet that appears as an Ibis-headed human or a baboon. He was considered the embodiment of all sciences and literature achievements. Djehuti was associated with sacred writing called Mdw Ntr pronounced Medu Netcher meaning sacred writings or divine thoughts.

You will see that Djehuti sometimes sits on the scales of justice in the process of the Weighing of the Heart. When a person has made the transition from life, she/he/they are judged on whether they have led a good life in trying to help others, and Djehuti in the form of a baboon will sometimes sit at the center of the scales of justice on the top as the balance. Baboons are highly intelligent and care for each other. Sometimes, it will be Maat who sits on the scales of Justice. The person's heart is weighed against Maat's feather of truth. Djuhuti is also in the form of the Ibis-headed divinity of the sacred word. He is a record keeper and stands with a notepad and paper and writes down the history and results of the weighing of the heart against Maat's feather of truth.

The written words of Kemet were the first classical evidence of writings and influenced the development of writings all over the world. That is not to say that symbols that appeared in caves and rocks all over the world by the original Africans who populated the world and became the First

Nations and diaspora of Africa were not writings and beautiful expressions of existence. Indeed, these early symbols were the bedrock of the later Mdw Ntr of Kemet.

Kemet was matriarchal: That is, the women and men were respected equally in status carrying out equally empowering roles. They sought to create harmony in their relationships as they were invested in producing harmonious families, and being good examples of the mothers and fathers, aunties, uncles, cousins, sisters, brothers, and eventually the elders. They wished to be examples of good people. The divinities created in Kemet were women and men, and they often came into the world together such as Djehuti who was accompanied by Seshat. At different historical moments, the pairings change although pairings remain reflective of African matriarchal beliefs.

The educator teaches the children the meaning of knowledge. One is trying ultimately to know self, and to acquire self-knowledge is the most important knowledge. This knowledge is a step toward enlightenment. Written on the temples in Kemet is the wisdom that instructs us to "Know thyself." When we can answer the questions "Who am I?" "Where am I?" "How did I get here?", we are on the path to knowing self. Knowing self is both internal as well as external. Most importantly, it is of the mind. The mind in ancient Africa is associated with the spirit, heart, and soul.

Knowledge: While knowledge is associated with philosophies usually those of the European cultural orientation beginning with the Greek, the earliest ones on which Greek philosophies are based, come out of Africa, Kemet in particular, because they are codified-written and thus viewed as genuine. Overall and simply, knowledge is culturally informed and produced. Knowledge is related to experience and learned. It is based on fact and truth. It is preserved by civilizations as it is the basis of their existence. There may be a question on what is knowledge if civilizations can contradict each other's knowledge base? In this work, we use the most ancient of knowledge that we know of and we can contrast and compare. Since we know that race is a falsehood, knowledge that is grounded in such ideas is not really based on truth and thus is not knowledge. It is information. Knowledge in Kemet means truth. One does not necessarily discount information that is false because even within the falsehood, there may be seeds of truth. However, one must be careful to be discriminatory when judging what is knowledge, for our very lives depend on knowledge which is truth. It is part of our consciousness where facts, beliefs, concepts, theories, images, ideas, opinions, suppositions, etc. live in our minds. Our minds can encompass both truth and lies, and that is why the Afrocentric model of education encourages us to develop critical minds.

Using Djehuti as a symbol to encourage knowledge-seeking and literacy in the classroom.

The image of Djehuti and his role in recording how near or far one is to keeping Maat alive in the heart of people making the transition from life to the next life or end if the Divine devourer Ammet or Ammut or Ammit (there were no vowels in Mdw Ntr so choices are made by those decipher) eats the corrupted evil heart; it is important to remind us in the classroom of our mission as humans to know or come to know who we are from an African perspective.

A simple course on understanding the specificity of knowledge and its importance may be used to explain. The following books are helpful: George James, *Stolen Legacy* (1989); Theophile Obenga, *African Philosophy*; Molefi Kete Asante, *The Egyptian Philosophers*.

You may look at the African philosophers and what they believed. Divide the class into three groups that align with three chosen African philosophers:

1. Imhotep on the Emergence of Reason
2. Ptahhotep and the Moral Order
3. Merikare on Common Sense

You will find these philosophers in *The Egyptian Philosophers* by Molefi Kete Asante, the father of Afrocentricity.

This work is Philosophy and Logic combined with Rhetoric.

4. Seshat

- **Definition:** Seshat is the feminine counterpart of Djehuti, associated with wisdom, writing and sacred architecture.

She is the divinity of books and libraries. Seshat holds a palm frond, which is recognized as a measuring tool used to create the foundations for building sacred buildings like temples and libraries. Another important work of Seshat was one of bookkeeping where she was a record keeper, an overseer of maintaining societal needs and therefore a mathematician. Seshat and Djehuti followed the principles of the seven liberal arts. In this way, as keepers of wisdom and knowledge they understand fully the seven liberal arts, which are connected and represent the path to education and thus to enlightenment. The intention is to achieve an education that can free the soul. If one understands that the mind is connected to the heart and soul, then knowledge, which is truth, has the potential of enlightenment that is reaching a high level of thought and understanding of the meaning of life. Djehuti and Seshat are skilled in these areas.

- **Context: The seven liberal arts**

1   Language Arts: The recognition that speech itself was sacred as was the expression of it in writing. The Mdw Ntr (Kemetic text) literarily the Divine word. Words create vibrations and writing was a way to express and interpret those vibrations through the development of symbols that could send their messages to us in through sight if we had sight. Many writings were carved, and those without sight could touch them and feel the meanings.

2. Rhetoric: The oratory of sound considered the study of the technique of using speech. It was an art form of using the voice and its vibrational sound to heal. The concept of good speech and righteous speech is linked to the vibrations of sound. Correct speech or truth speech produced harmony.

3. Logic: The study of the interpretation of theory, subject, and matter. The mind—thought can investigate and determine the truth or falsehood of the theory. Logic is based on truth and without truth there is only illogical, which may pass for logic in those who do not have knowledge.

4. Mathematics: The study of numbers, configurations, quantity, shape, space, and the metaphysics of being. Metaphysics is the study of reality, existence, life, our spiritual relationship to the universe.

5. Geometry: The branch of mathematics concerned with the properties, relationships, and of points, lines, curves, and surfaces.

6. Astronomy: The scientific study of celestial bodies and the universe, not separated from our planet and galaxy. It branches into astrometry, astrodynamics, cosmology, and astrophysics. The study looks at the measurements and the positions of body space as well as seeking to find their properties and origins.

7. The arts: Music in particular is considered to be the living practice of philosophy: the route to harmony with nature, the celestial bodies, divinities, and used to cure disease.

The importance of these two divinities is to view them as embodying the skills of each other into one composite whole that becomes one. Noting the complementarity of the divinities as female and male assists in highlighting the importance of women in knowledge creation and education.

Creative writing projects can be developed, inspired by Seshat's legacy as a divinity critical in the building of sacred buildings.

Seshat wears a band on her head from which rises a star with seven points. She also wears a panther skin as part of her sacred priestess regalia, which was an important part of the rituals used in buildings. The panther skin was worn by priestesses and priests. It was a symbol of power, protection, and royalty. Note that the panther is a Black leopard. We may think of how important the Black Panther movement was in the United States. It led to extended human rights for Black people in the cities throughout the country who were being harassing, killed, and imprisoned for being Black by the police. Women were the majority of Black Panthers. A good film is Black Panthers: Vanguard of the Revolution" (https://www.youtube.com/watch?v=bqxwTABwtnU&t=112s).

Learning how culture is transmitted generationally can explain how people can still remember parts (vestiges) of their ancient past. The Black Panther was chosen in the United States by ordinary people to represent the human rights movement of the Black communities because the panther only fights in defense. Perhaps the people knew of the panthers' significant sacred status in ancient Africa where it also lives as a free animal. At one time during the European colonization and conquest of Africa, millions of animals like the panthers were hunted and killed as trophies and their skins were used as fashionable clothing that only the wealthy could afford. Nations like the Zulu of South Africa use the skin in traditional dress for sacred occasions to this day.

The significance of writing, Maat and the notion of divine women from Kemet, provides examples of the obligation to write in truth. The earliest writings were considered words of truth and thus divine. The symbols of writing represented symbols of truth. The book *Daughters of Africa: An International Anthology of Words and Writings by Women of African Descent from Ancient Egyptian to the Present* by Margaret Busby is a must-have for the Afrocentric educator to use for the pupils. This beautiful book holds the writings of women who changed the world through their thoughts, writings, and activism. Hatshepsut, daughter of Thutmose I, was a Per aa from the eighteenth dynasty who ruled from 1490 to 1469 BCE. She wrote of her love for Amun—a word for God or the divine energy of life—and how she had practiced Maat in her lifetime. See pages 12–14. Also during her reign Per aa Hatshepsut designed and built her magnificent mortuary temple.

Women writers like Alice Walker, Angela Davis, and Maya Angelou are there among many others. Interviews on YouTube with some of these great women writers and poets, etc. can be an inspiration to all children. The reading of their works with the understanding that they are carrying on the cultural heritage of African women's power, without fear in a racist patriarchal culture, which attempts to undermine the agency of women, in particular the darker and darkest skin women. In some religions, these women are still viewed as property through enslavement in modern religions.

Teachers could give prizes to great storytellers like those in the lesson plans. The pupils can narrate their own stories to their classes and then to present them to the whole school and other schools on Zoom at interschool gatherings, which can spread to the rest of the world.

The idea of knowing the partnership of knowledge and wisdom between Djehuti and Seshat is to understand that writing was invented by matriarchal Africans and that it was used to convey knowledge and express the thoughts from our minds to solve solutions and create a better world through the sciences.

This work is Language arts combined with Philosophy and Logic.

5. Maaticity

- **Definition:** The process of living according to the principles of Maat.
  - o   Encouraging students to reflect on fairness, balance, and reciprocity in their daily interactions.

The children can provide examples of people who sought to be Maatic in the way that they lived their lives. There are people who know nothing of the ancient divinity of Maat but lived according to the seven major principles: Truth, Justice, Reciprocity, Righteousness, Harmony, Balance, and Order. These people might be like the elderly grandmother who lived down the street and always watched the children and street happenings and made sure that everything was right and spoke kindly to everyone and made people feel better no matter what type of day that they had to face. Although the priestesses and priests were trained to be the very best of humans who could care for their communities and heal, there were people who were not necessarily trained but lived in Maat as they knew it as members of societies that highlighted the need to seek and maintain peace, love, compassion, and harmonious relations.

In class discussion, the pupils may provide examples of people whom they know or have known that embrace Maaticity in their everyday lives. Questions around why the examples have been chosen, or what do they do or what have they done that qualifies them to be Maatic. They do not need to exist today; they may have made a transition to ancestorhood and are no longer with us. These examples may be from our families, from our communities, from history, from any place in the world, people we have met and made us feel better, joyful, or happy when we felt sad. There are many examples, and there is no limitation once there is an understanding of the principles of Maat.

This work is Language arts.

6. Complementarity

- **Definition:** Female and male balance based on reciprocity

A cultural system emphasizing balanced roles and mutual respect between genders. This idea rises out of the two-cradle theory of Cheikh Anta Diop who recognized the significance of culture to life. There are essentially two major cultures in the world. The positioning of the woman as mother defines the major differences in these two cultures. When the woman as the potential mother is respected and appreciated, that cultural orientation will produce complementary relationships among humans that are respectful and harmonious. This is African matriarchy where hierarchies of superiority and inferiority are not encouraged.

The second major culture Patriarchy is thousands of years younger than African matriarchy. Patriarchy disrespects the woman as potential mother, and she is viewed as biologically and mentally inferior to the man as potential father. This hierarchy of man as superior to woman is the first recognized social injustice. The woman is not inferior to the man. Out of this cultural orientation, there is always hierarchy. The hierarchy of humanity comes from this belief. Humans are considered superior of inferior based on skin color. The belief in the superiority and inferiority based on skin color is racist and based on a belief that there are at least five races of human beings. The belief in races, Polygenesis, is a pseudo-scientific belief that has been shown to be scientifically untrue. There is only one race, and that is humanity. The belief in race arises from the belief in the European doctrine of white supremacy. Although it is not true, millions believe in this doctrine, and to this day, this belief dictates what type of life one might lead. There are essentially five so-called races whereby based on skin color, she, he, and they are deemed to be either superior or inferior. This belief is based on a doctrine called white supremacy, which manifests in European culture. It is ethnocentric, rising from Ethnography, which is originally the science of the description and classification of the races of mankind. Since there is only one human race, it tends to reify a belief that must be dismantled, particularly as it is a falsehood and millions of people have been murdered because of this belief. This belief is hierarchical and the opposite of complementarity, which highlights the reciprocal, harmonious, and balanced relationship that members of African matriarchal societies seek to develop and maintain.

- **Context:**

Discussions on gender equity must be inclusive of the construction of race as they are not separate, but are synchronous, in that one led to the other. Understanding intersectionality will be important for viewing the relationship between patriarchy and race when investigating the place of women in society. At the same time, it is useful as a concept to understand the different forms of hierarchy that can impact on one person, for example, being a dark skin girl who comes from Haiti, with one parent, who is middle class and lives in area where the majority of people are impoverished and the major language is not French, and the people are phenotypically lighter and believe in race inferiority and superiority like the people in the Dominican Republic who are predominantly light skin and speak Spanish and are guilty of killing dark skin Haitian people. That is the problem of feminism while it is biologically determined, and it does not equate its own historical cultural and theoretical role in the belief in and practice of race and white supremacy. This makes it more difficult to confront racism when one practices it. Womanism was created by a Black woman Alice Walker who did not believe that she could link herself to feminism because it believes in the race paradigm and practitioners have a history of racism. African womanism recognizes the African origin of civilization in that all our ancestors are African and Black and that African matriarchy produced the first civilized behaviors that strove to produce complementary relations and societies that could create true democratic ideals, which are Maatic.

The students may discuss examples of intersectionality, looking at its roots in law and the meaning of law and its relationship to justice and truth.

This work is theory and Logic.

7. Ga Nation

- **Definition:** A nation of people living in Ghana

The Ga nation is in Ghana known for its spiritual and cultural traditions. The Ga language is a Sudanese language or language of Kush, which is older than Sudan. It has been argued linguistically that the Ga traveled from Kemet to the West coast of Africa the area later called the "gold coast" by European enslavers and colonizers. It was renamed Ghana when Kwame Nkrumah became the first African leader of this Western government. Ghana was an ancient civilization that existed at the same time as Kemet. According to the important work of Kwame Osei, who wrote *The Ancient Egyptian Origins of English Languages*, argued that the Ga and Akan nations migrated from Kemet. They still have names like Ankrah, Ankh meaning life and Ra or Rah referring to the Divinity Ra—another name for God or the sun which is also viewed as divine as there can be no life without it.

- **Context**

Because the education model is Afrocentric, there is no hierarchy regarding the significance of nations. There are many nations in Africa, some alienated from each other and practicing anti-African beliefs resulting from Arabic and European colonization and enslavement that have prevented the cultural transmission of values and beliefs of the conquered and indigenous people. Cultural relocation is the attempt to reawaken the cultural memory through education and knowledge as the basis for cultural identity. This book is an attempt to do so. As we come to know our cultural history, we can begin to identify similarities among nations regarding some of the ancient traditions such as respect for:

- Women as babies, girls, leaders, and mothers. In some nations, each girl child may be born into a women's group.
- For the children. One of the most important skills a child will learn is how to care for younger siblings. A Kongo proverb says: "Whoever never babysat will never understand the beauty of life and that of parenting."
- The Elders. The elders hold wisdom, and they teach the families the cultural history of events that happened before they were born. In this way, they will know who they are and their responsibilities to their families and co-families.
- The Ancestors. The ancestors are revered for their contribution to the families. They are remembered as those who were good and made the world a better place for the families to live. One cannot become an ancestor if one does not try to improve self, family, community, and nations during life. To become an ancestor is a high honor as it is only bestowed upon those who will be remembered as good, kind, loving, compassionate people.

Using a map of Africa before conquest and one after can show the pupils how the culture through colonization and enslavement affected relationships among nations, institutions, organizations, and beliefs through different languages, religions, and borders imposed.

The history of the Ga people can be examined looking at cultural practices to teach respect for African diversity and heritage. From research carried out in Ghana, the Ga parents who live in the urban old town setting traditionally have separate homes. The children are raised among the women family members until 5 to 6 years and then the boys go to their father's house to be raised to understand their roles as men.

Discussion and acting out what values can be taught that are significant to girls and boys. Can this be done in a U.S. setting? At one time in Africa, both girls and boys learned how to become responsible adults through the teachings of rites of passage, a physical, spiritual, and metaphysical undertaking to help the children learn their responsibilities to their nations. What can be taught to children with the principles of Maat and the search for harmony and balance? The pupils can be formed into groups to come up with ideas of gender roles. In Africa, gender is not rigid as practiced in the United States and other Europeanized countries. People will do what is necessary to keep the societies working. If a farming family in the rural area raise cattle and the boys traditionally do this work, then if a cattle-raising family has only girls, the girls will raise the cattle. It will be the same with household chores or skills like cooking, farming, animal husbandry, weaving, gold working, teaching, healing, writing, artisanry, architecture, and sciences.

A powerful example of how this gender fluidity worked in the United States was during the European world wars of I and II, while the men fought in battle, the women ran the institutions of the countries. This happened in the United States, and we may see how it took place in the film called *Six Triple Eight* on Netflix. It stars Kerry Washington, highlighting the true story of African American women who wanted to fight in battle, and there is a long history of women warriors in Africa, but instead were sent to England to sort the mail for the U.S. soldiers and their families. The African American women soldiers sorted mail that had not been sent for years, which lay abandoned and helped military families know what happened to their loved ones, how they felt, and the losses and loves between families. While the racism and patriarchy looked down on Black women, they created a working postal system where the men and their families could receive their mail.

The pupils may choose writers and read their works and review them. Their findings will be shared in the class and they each can develop a presentation with or without a PowerPoint slide show to explain the findings of their reviews.

This area of development would fall under Language arts.

8. Nubia/Kush

- **Definition:** A region in southern Egypt and northern Sudan known for its contributions to African civilizations.

Nubia also known earlier as Kush played a powerful role in the creation of Kemet. Bones found in Kush and Kemet showed that the earlier people of Kemet were the same as the current people of Kush. As we have learned, Ta Seti was pre-Kemet. The Kushites were always matriarchal, and over time, the invasions of the patriarchal Hyksos, Persians, Assyrians, Greeks, Romans and Arabic people made Kemet more patriarchal. The Kushites retired to a homeland bordered by Kemet, called Kush then is now called Sudan. They entered Kemet in the 25th dynasty and stayed for 100 years. The 25th dynasty brought back women as leaders in key political positions. Importantly, Kush located in today's Sudan is remembered for the warriorship of the Kandake Queen Amanitore who lived from 40 to 10 BCE and led women warriors against the Romans from 25 to 22 BCE who had conquered Kemet after the death of Cleopatra VII in 30 BCE. Eventually, the Arabs would take Kemet and Kush, and the English and Arab conquerors would call Kush Sudan.

There are PowerPoints that can provide the images and information of this historical time, relating Africa to Kemet and Kush and present-day Sudan. The women of Kush now Sudan are enslaved and forbidden to speak their indigenous language. They were once warriors. The film "I am slave" is an important film that shows how modern-day Kushite-Nubian women are enslaved to rich Arabic people and travel to European countries as "servants" and "help" (https://www.youtube.com/watch?v=HEBxuNYmbXI).

This work is Language and arts.

9. Krio

- **Definition:** A language and African group in Sierra Leone formed from:

Africans freed from enslavement by supporting George III of Britain and his Black wife of German and Portuguese descent, Charlotte of England, during the American Civil War between 1861 and 1865. Charlotte gave birth to 15 children and forbade the royal household from purchasing and eating sugar in support of those African people enslaved in the sugar plantations of the Americas, including Caribbean islands. These freed Africans from North America, which became the United States after the war of independence from Britain, were known as Loyalists.

Some Africans left Britain to pursue a new life in Freetown Sierra Leone as part of a British plan to evacuate Black people and send them "home" to Africa. Many of those who arrived on the first ships from Britain died, and some of the free African men had European wives and they had children.

African people captured on the West coast, who were freed from ships carrying them to enslavement in other parts of the world.

West Africans who journeyed to develop Freetown created a new nation of people who included Europeans (mainly women, the wives), Africans who were freed in different ways, indigenous African people from the area and those who migrated from other parts of West Africa, perhaps escaping enslavement or persecution or traveling to forge a new life. They formed the Krio nation and spoke a linguistic mixture of the African languages encompassed.

The book *Black and British: A forgotten History* by David Olusoga and the documentary film series based on this book is powerful and relevant to the story of the Krio people of Sierra Leone who landed in a place they named Freetown.

Prior to the arrival of the Krio and their determination to establish a settlement whose name reflected the belief in the freedom of African people who had escaped from the terrors of Jamaica, the United States and enslavement boats were routed to these destinations, as well as local people and those who traveled looking for safe places: Some who went to Freetown were members of families that had been captured and enslaved in Sierra Leone. The first fortress in Sierra Leone to imprison captured enslaved African people was built in Bunce Island in 1670 by the British and destroyed and rebuilt by the French and pirates contesting for the profits made from this shameful business. Tens of thousands of Africans were forcefully shipped to the American colonies. Many were sold on the Island to slavers of every phenotype relishing in the profits made. Most clearly their cultural beliefs no matter what phenotypes brought them together in inhuman profit-making deals based on the supposed worth of these African women, men, and children. The Geechee Gullah people enslaved on Jekyll Island, one of the islands off the Georgia coast, are said to have come from Sierra Leone. This was discovered because of the similarity in their basketry skills.

- **Context:**

Linking Krio's history to lessons on resilience and cultural synthesis. Even today one can visit the Georgia coast and Jekyll Island and see the ancient oak trees with Spanish moss growing on them, where Africans created community. The Geechee Gullah people still retain some of the African languages that they brought with them. The pupils can use Geography to show the distance between Sierra Leone and Jekyll Island and what it took to survive the journey as captured enslaved people whose enslavement would continue 50 years after enslavement was officially abolished in 1865.

The film "Daughters of the Dust" by Julie Dash who is part of the LA rebellion film movement that included the Ethiopian film maker, Haile Gerima, who made the film "Sankofa" provided a new cultural way of looking at Black people. They brought African cultural history into the lives of the characters in their stories, creating a new sensitivity regarding cultural transmission of values and beliefs that brought the Africanness back into the picture. This new phase in filmmaking can be especially exciting for the pupils to investigate. Some of the members of the LA rebellion were Charles Burnett, Billy Woodberry, Jamaa Fanaka, Barbara McCullough, Larry Clark, Alile Sharon Larkin, Ben Caldwell, and Zeinabu Irene Davis. Finding out who they are and what films they made would encourage the thoughts of potential young film makers. Beyonce's film "Lemonade" was made by Julie Dash and was reminiscent of "Daughters of the Dust" (https://www.youtube.com/watch?v=1Ket0T3zWwc&t=136s). It would inspire the making of film makers and the dramatic arts and others in the class who have playwriting skills.

This work is the Arts.

10. Ankrah

- **Definition:** A name notable of lineage among the Ga people of Ghana.
- **Context:**
  o   Using Ankrah's history to illustrate African heritage and identity.

O. Kwame Osei is a linguist and historian who traced the journey of the Ga and the Akan from Kemet to Ghana through the language that retains some of the words of Kemet. Ankhra or Ankra or Ankrah are names that include two terms, the Ankh meaning life and Rah or Ra meaning God or the sun without which we cannot exist. Thus, Ankrah means in the living image of God or the living God. This name is linked more to the priest and priestess role of those who bear the name from ancient times. Sometimes we bear names, and yet, we have no knowledge of their meaning, and the responsibilities attached to the names. All names have meaning. The book by O. Kwame Osei is called *The Ancient Egyptian Origins of the English Language*. It traces language and names to the early Europeans who were still phenotypically Black Africans. He uses Stonehenge, one of the oldest sites of the stone calendars considered 4,000 years old as a site that may have been built by the Kemites, and we may surmise that we can look at such sites as culturally relevant to people, society, nation, Nation state. Namoratunga in Northwestern Kenya is an archaeo astronomical megalithic stone site dated 300 BCE, which is oriented toward the stars. Today, we have found Inzala yelanga, in Mpumalanga in South Africa, which is indeed the oldest stone calendar which has been dated most recently to possibly 200,000 years old. This ancient model can show that Stonehenge, like Namoratunga, is culturally African as O. Kwame Osei surmised. Pictures can be found.

The Book of African Names by Molefi Kete Asante is an attempt to help parents choose their children's names, to help us choose new names, and to inform us about the meaning of the names that we might already have. When the conquerors come to take the lands from the people, they give new names to locations and the people so they will forget their past and accept the new names, in time, as the original names. In this way, there is no memory of the past and we lose our cultural identity. As a linguist, O. Kwame Osei is able to define the African presence in Europe and the Americas. We know that there is a relationship with Africa as Africans migrated out of Africa 50 to 70,000 years ago and populated the world and became the first indigenous people, the First Nations people, and the Diaspora of humanity. Like O. Kwame Osei, Cheikh Anta Diop, Ivan Van Sertima and his team of scientists, archaeologists, astronomers, linguists, anthropologists, historians and writers, etc., who published in the *Journal of African Civilizations*, we are seeking and finding connections.

In relation to the names, the students in the classroom collective may choose names that they feel suit them by using the book by Molefi Kete Asante. They are playing, so they do not need to force anyone to rename them unless there is some agreement with the families. The book shows the areas in Africa from which the names arose and exactly their meanings. The students can have a fun day choosing names. Keep in mind that our ancestors are originally from Africa, and we are the descendants and may choose names that address our places in the family and who we think we are and who we think we may become.

11. Asa G. Hilliard III's Questions

- **Definition:** Three critical questions for self-awareness—Who am I? Where am I? How on earth did I get here?

Incorporating these reflective questions into classroom discussions about identity and history can take place after undergoing a process of knowledge development. The discussion would begin with an overall understanding of culture and its role in developing identity. If one is prevented from knowing one's culture, there is a problem in knowing who one is as culture transmits this information. In the process of conquest as with the First Nations people of the Americas, the taking of their lands in conquest included the necessary prevention of their own cultural knowledge. In the United States and Canada, as well as places like Australia, hundreds of thousands of children, perhaps millions were cruelly ripped away from their families and taken to schools across the country far from their homes to be taught how to be white, a manifestation of the race doctrine. They were considered red in the Americas and Black in Australia. Here, the belief in race justified this cruel procedure to remove children from their families and societies and stop their cultural knowledge transmission. Many of these children died after living in these boarding schools and were buried in the school grounds. New discoveries are still being made. The delicate beautiful children were treated with abuse and hatred, and they were depressed and unable to be themselves and experience love, happiness, and peace within themselves. They could not understand what was happening to them. They no longer knew who they were, where they were, and how they got to where they were. The truth and logic of their societies were no longer available to them.

Asa Hilliard was an educational psychologist and knew that to be a balanced functioning person, all people need to know who they are, where they are, and how they got anywhere. It does not mean that they cannot function without this knowledge, but it means that they can function better with it. We particularly understand this condition with children who are considered lessor or inferior in a society that professes to be righteous and just, to all and applies race, relating to the amount of melanin in the skin, to view the intellectual, psychological, attitudinal, moral, educational capacity of the child. The racialization of humanity has enforced untruths of notions of inferiority and superiority upon everyone. Children entering any Eurocentric institutes of education, no matter in what country they exist, are taught that their racialization in a hierarchy based on notions of inferiority or superiority, is part of a natural order. Their supposed inferiority or superiority based on skin color is normalized to the degree that although it is a lie, children can feel a measure of security because this is all that they know, or in some cases, have ever known. It is not only in the schooling system that they are entering to learn who they are not, but it is promoted in modern religions which some may believe in, and every institution that has been created to reflect the values and beliefs of a culture that believes in race. What happened to the red people of the Americas, whose land we live on in the United States, appears perfectly normalized as we are accustomed to not knowing what happened to them or if we know something, they deserved to not be here any longer as is the case of the First Nations people in the Caribbean. These false ideas are not healthy for any child. The seven principles of Maat, Truth, Justice, Righteousness, Reciprocity, Harmony, Balance, and Order do not exist in their teaching. Isfet the opposite of Maat represents injustice, lies, unrighteous, unreciprocated, imbalance, disharmonious, and chaos. To move toward Maat, the Afrocentric teacher is provided the power to make the changes necessary to dismantle and thus transform the education system. A priority is helping the child to understand the truth of "who am I," "where am I," and "how did I get here?" Literally, one does not ask the child these questions, and it is the responsibility of the educator to provide the knowledge of the chronological history of humanity to enable a child, she, he, and they to understand who they are, as they do not understand in the first place the process of cultural suppression and dislocation that they are going through, or the cultural retention and vestiges that they possess, whatever phenotype they represent, as there is no framework for them to assess the condition. The Afrocentric model of education is used to provide the knowledge necessary to begin the deconstruction process toward what we may call "optimal psychology" as professed by Linda James Myers.

12. Kemetic Philosophy (Seba and Sebait)

- **Definition:** These two words refer to the wise and the teaching of wisdom.

Seba means "Wise" and Sebait means "Wisdom" and thus the art of Wisdom Teaching which is the basis of "Deep Thought." One may understand that deep thought is linked to becoming conscious and the "unconscious" of humanity as suggested by Edward Bruce Bynum and Linda James Myers in the book *Our African Unconscious: The Black Origins of Mysticism and Psychology*. This is evident in matriarchal societies like the First Nations people in Australia who highly value wisdom and elevate those whom they call "Keepers of Wisdom." Essentially, the status of keepers of wisdom is linked to ancestral connections and the transmission of cultural knowledge maintained intergenerationally as a critical component of cultural memory.

The Greek word philosophy that we use is neither rooted in the Greek language nor in the Indo-Aryan language that Greek is rooted in, according to Theophile Obenga the student of Cheikh Anta Diop. He reasons that philosophy does not have a Greek etymology because the Greeks went to Kemet for the knowledge and wisdom. Currently, we recognize that philosophy was the expression or term learned from the ancient word Sebait. Philos means friendship, love, and attraction, and Sophia means wisdom, knowledge, and intelligence. Thus, together the word philosophy is the love of wisdom and knowledge. Those dedicated to that tradition learned Sebait from Kemet where people from all over the world went to learn the knowledge of African people. Ancient African teachings emphasized the need to understand and live in Maat as a way of ethical living, critical thinking, and harmony. Sebait was scientific and metaphysical.

- **Context:**

Designing lessons that foster wisdom and ethical reasoning in students.

The first lesson for the child is to understand what philosophy is, especially its history. In the words of Molefi Kete Asante "the understanding of philosophy is well articulated: The antiquity of African philosophy is unique and stand alone and is older than all other philosophies. While civilizations such as the Sumerian and Minoan produced pottery, vases and frescoes during the period of the earliest Egyptian dynasties, only Egypt produced a body of work consistent enough to be ethical, spiritual, and moral aspects to be called philosophy. It would be much later, nearly two thousand years, before the Greeks, who were influenced by the Egyptians, would develop their own philosophy. My aim is to introduce the reader to the earliest understandings of the human experience, birth, life, death, the good, the just, and the beautiful ... The ancient Africans of the Nile Valley believed that knowledge was the way to life and the way to life led directly to the divine. Inner knowledge came from the search for the divine and wisdom was the result of inner knowledge."

Vimbai Chivaura, a Zimbabwean educator, activist, theologian, was compassionate and good and believed in the traditional Shona religion. He studied how can Africans in Zimbabwe care for their people given that the farms were owned by the European conquerors. At that time, some European farmers released their farms to the government in support of the idea. The majority fought to maintain control of the farms despite calls to enact decolonization. Vimbai Chivaura believed that philosophy is what African people on the continent think so much about, that it is like breathing. In some ways, he thought that it could not be a discipline separated from the living of life. It was in essence the discovery of the meaning of life sought by all people who all possess the wisdom to access knowledge—truth.

All philosophical thoughts are grounded in culturally oriented theories. For instance, if one thinks that civilization began when white men ruled as patriarchs, then the philosophies will reflect the kinds of thoughts that will arise from this falsehood. Thoughts based on such falsehood will attempt to justify the behaviors that could make this condition righteous and appear true. If they become "true," they are seen to be based on "logic." However, it is not possible to have logic without truth; thus, a false "truth" creates illogicity among those who believe it. There were thousands of years of civilization and thus philosophy relating to African matriarchal beliefs that achieved respect and complementarity in status, which were reflected in governing structures from the local to the national representing the voice of the people. Councils of Elders and women, etc., from villages to towns were formulated to feed into the greater governing structure of the Nation state of Kemet as well as societies across Africa. From the Eurocentric perspective, it is difficult to believe that thousands of years ago there was any person, he, she, or they, on earth capable of thinking, let alone higher thinking. Part of the reason for this problem of cultural thought is that it is based on false historical information used to justify ownership of knowledge viewed as though based on truth. The challenges to this supposed "truth" arise from the victims whose truth has been denied and hidden. Their voices have not and cannot be heard so that any challenge to the falsehood is removed and viewed as truth. Philosophy plays a large role in this. To study Kemetic philosophy is based on the knowledge that philosophies from

Kemet were culturally matriarchal, always seeking Maat, as foundational to civilization. Such ideas stand in opposition to the Eurocentric academic belief that patriarchy and thus race were the beginning of civilization.

We may use the following books to learn the teachings of the ancient African philosophers, *The Egyptian Philosophers: Ancient African Voices from Imhotep to Akhenaten*, Theophile Obenga's book, *African Philosophy*, Maulana Karenga's book, *Selections from the Husia, Sacred Wisdom of Ancient Egypt*, and *SBA: The Reawakening of the African Mind* by Asa G. Hilliard. The lecture in the following video will help in the instructions: https://www.youtube.com/watch?v=RQGU2TSTo0A&t=530s

This course will fit into language arts.

13. Cheikh Anta Diop's Cradle Theory

- **Definition:** A theory distinguishing cultural orientations of humanity's "southern cradle" (Africa) and "northern cradle" (Europe).
- **Context:**

Cheikh Anta Diop: A multi-genius and visionary for humanity. He studied nuclear physics, chemistry African history, Egyptology, linguistics, anthropology. Diop fought always for the integrity, character, and beauty of Africa to be re-known. Born in Diourbel, Senegal, in 1923, he entered Ancestorhood in 1986. Cheikh Anta Diop used African cultural knowledge based on the scientific achievements of African people on the continent, to evaluate his studies and skills in linguistics, cultural and physical anthropology, history, chemistry physics, and Egyptology. From his research, he understood that culture affected the minds and behaviors of humans and that there were essentially two major cultures in existence that he could identify that were almost in opposition to one another. He noted that the original culture, which came from Africa in time branched into a new culture. Although his work may be termed Afrocentric as he placed Africa in the center of his understanding of humanity, because Africa was the birthplace of humanity.

Using the model of the seven liberal arts, which although often studied as distinct disciplines today, are in fact part of a whole that the ancient educators viewed as the educational path to attaining enlightenment.

As it was with the integration of the disciplines that Cheikh Anta Diop attained, he brought the disciplines together to form a holistic approach to his study. This is much like the attempt in the book *The Afrocentric School [a blueprint]* to imitate this style of learning. The Two-Cradle Theory was the outcome of this massive research over the disciplines.

Cheikh Anta Diop laid out a theory that can be and has been built upon by Diopian theorists. Some of us failed to admit the influence of his work on their own work, some have tried to undermine his work and his character. In the case of this book, Diop has been key to the development of the Afrocentric model of Education that is being developed in this work. In answer to Molefi Kete Asante's question at a personal meeting with Cheikh Anta Diop in Dakar, where he asked what he could do to help Africa, Diop stated "Africa does not need help, Advance, Advance, Advance." This idea is that we build upon the "knowledge" or "episteme" or "truth" that he gave us and build upon it. This is what has happened. African Womanism as Afrocentric theory is grounded in the Two-Cradle Theory as that is the African origin of humanity, matriarchy, and the respect of women as potential mothers. This is the Afrocentric framework to this book.

The ideas of the Two-Cradle Theory are that there are essentially two cradles of civilization, and their differences are distinguished by the relationship between the woman and man, the mother and father who produce life and culture. He surmised correctly based on science that:

- The Southern Cradle—Africa is the birthplace of Humanity.
- Cultural unity in Africa exists and this unity is critical to developing a better future in Africa and therefore the world.
- Cultural identity formation is critical to developing cultural unity.

The work of Cheikh Anta Diop is critical as Afrocentric theory is the foundation of the education model that is being designed in this work. The two-cradle theory is pivotal to understanding cultural distinctions among people. The movement of people out of Africa helps to create an inclusionary model of education, in that humanity was born in Africa and that all humans have African and Black ancestors.

All humans' mitochondrial DNA traces back to one African mother from the Southern Cradle. Scientifically, as human types, we are known as *Homo sapiens*. We are at least 350,000 years old.

Humans did not leave the Southern cradle until 70,000 years ago.

- Africa produced the first culture.
- The first culture, born in the Southern Cradle of Civilization, was grounded in female–male reciprocity.
- Female–male reciprocity/harmony is called African matriarchy in this model as it does not subscribe to the European notion of matriarchy as representative of the domination of the woman by the man.
- African matriarchal culture produced the divinity and ethical and moral substance of Maat (the Divine Mother).
- African matriarchy expresses respect and love of and for the woman as mother.
- Mothering in Africa is considered a high-ideal status.
- Anyone who is loving and compassionate can be considered a mother, regardless of gender.
- Ancient spiritual systems exemplify the indivisibility of female–male as creator.
- Nonhierarchical—Egalitarian—Democratic—Balanced.
- A person is judged by what she, he, they contribute to the world.
- Ancestral recognition and respect is foundational.
- Some Africans left the Southern Cradle 70,000 years ago. African people populated the world and became the First Nations people and the Diaspora.
- Environments developed new phenotypes.
- Over time, the culture of African matriarchy changed, linked to environmental causation and new patterns in behaviors and beliefs evolving into patriarchy, which is the domination of the woman (mother) by the man (father).
- Patriarchal culture stands in opposition to African matriarchal culture as it clearly challenges ideas of Maat through hierarchy and injustice the basis of this sociocultural relational form.
- The opposite of Maat, meaning order, is Isfet, meaning chaos.
- The debasement of the African mother of humanity, regarding her biology and morality, is reflected in modern religions. The woman as potential mother is viewed as unfaithful to her husband, forming an alliance with the devil. She is considered biologically and morally inferior, the opposite of her status in African matriarchy.

At one time, the whole world was populated by African, dark-skinned humanity.

Over time and owing to harsh unmerciful climates, Africans lost touch with our African ancestors and created hierarchies of gender, race, caste, etc., justifying murder, genocide, rape, enslavement, colonization, and many forms of oppression. We can use the example of the Indo-Aryans who conquered the Harrapan civilization in India. The Indus Valley where the Harrapan civilization was located was a civilization that was matriarchal, had writing still undeciphered, and built as most amazing architecture, the remains of which are equal to those of Kemet. These Harrapan sometimes known as the Dasa have been linked to ancient Kushites, regarding their African beliefs and values. The Indo-Aryans as known, some of whom originated in the Steppes, conquered the Indus Valley civilization. From the research of the *Ancient Near East of Today*, an online digital platform of experts, one learns of "[t]he Indo-Aryans, from ca. 1500 BCE, crossed the Hindu Kush into the Indus valley, known in cuneiform texts as Meluuha, and defined the cultural and religious foundations of Hindu India." These are the conquerors of the dark skin African people of India in today's Pakistan who created Brahminism, one of the earliest evidences of the racialization of humanity ensconced in a religion believing in the inferiority of women and the darkest skin people (the Harrapan) and creating caste based on separate colors keeping the Blacks (the civilizers) at the base of a brutal unmerciful hierarchy. Please look at *Being Human Being* for more details in relation to how this ancient belief plays out in contemporary Indian society, for the "untouchables."

While we recognize that the people who inhabited the world migrated out of Africa, we recognize that over time, cultural differences occurred as well as phenotypical differences. In this educational model, it is argued that cultural differences outweigh physical differences and the idea of race as a genetic determiner of humanity. It is postulated and asserted that those who became patriarchal because of difficult times with sparse resources forgot their cultural knowledge of African matriarchy.

It is argued in this work that the patriarchal racists traveled the world and met their African ancestors whom they did not recognize. They would have revered them if they had not forgotten them. The culture of the Indo-Aryans or Indo Europeans noted as creators of patriarchal racist hierarchy in India starting out on the steppes have transmitted these values and beliefs for at least 4,000 years.

Those of the Northern cradle took advantage of the gentleness, knowledge, and higher learning of those who practiced African matriarchal values. To justify conquest and cruelty, they pretended that the people they met were inhuman, subhuman, uncivilized, base, demons, animals.

They were jealous of their accomplishments and beauty.

Northern cradle conquerors took from those who practiced African matriarchal values their sacred lands, possessions, wealth, knowledge, and untold lives.

Where these two cultures met, Diop called Zones of Confluence. We may say that the United States, India, Arabia, Australia, Israel, Canada, the Caribbean, South America all over Africa are zones of confluence where these cradles meet.

14. Ubuntu

- **Definition:** A South African philosophy meaning "I am because we are," emphasizing community and shared humanity.

Incorporating Ubuntu into classroom norms and group activities.

As Molefi Kete Asante teaches, the philosophy *Ubuntu* rises from the Bantu language. It is central to the way the 700 African nation groups in the east and south of Africa speak of relationships with each other. To have *Ubuntu* not unlike Maat means that you completely submit yourself to the social commitment of the people. This is a metaphysical commitment. One cannot escape from this social obligation except to declare oneself a heretic, outside of the body politic, foreign, oppositional, dangerous, and to be suspected. The Zulu say "*Umuntu ngumuntu ngabantu*" meaning that "I am because you are."

African philosophical beliefs reveal a fundamental allegiance to the collective ideals of community, not the self-centered individuality made so by one's own thinking reminiscent of the Northern cradle cultural beliefs. The focus on individuality is alien to African cultural beliefs that rather favor the collective agency of people. In this collective setting, the development of the individual is highly prized and encouraged among all members. Indeed, the agency of the community is enhanced by the development of individuals who hold allegiance to the community. When one speaks of communication, we speak beyond speech, we speak of intuition and metaphysical connections that humans make with one another, in that they "feel" relationships. In this way, one is speaking of one's relationship with *abantu*. I am not alone; if I seek to be alone, hinting that one is connected to one's ancestors and thus never alone. Desmond Tutu, the South African leader believed that in *Ubuntu* philosophy, "My humanity is bound up in yours, for we can only be human together."

15. Wayne Chandler's "Ancient Future"

- **Definition:** The idea of reconnecting with ancient knowledge to inform modern practices.

Wayne Chandler is an anthrophotojournalist researcher who has contributed to the excellent work of African discoveries in the *Journal of African Civilizations*, which was edited by Ivan Van Sertima. Wayne Chandler was one of the two researchers who discovered long-hidden photographs of the African Olmec giant stone heads found in Mexico in ancient America. On discovering this, Ivan Van Sertima invited Wayne Chandler to write for the journal and for the next 10 years contributed to locating important research. He was part of the team who worked with Ivan Van Sertima to find the African presence in ancient Europe, Asia, the East, ancient America, and so on. His own expertise is in India where his important writings and teachings reveal the roots of Brahminism, which is critical to our knowledge on understanding the cultural construction of race and racism through the Indo-Aryan conquest of the Harappan civilization. His wisdom is connected to ancient African wisdoms that he has found still practiced to some extent within ancient Indian wisdoms. Grounding in the higher learning of Kemet, which spread to India through the Kushites from the Nile Valley who created Ta Seti, he teaches us how to understand and apply higher learning techniques to our lives.

Wayne Chandler's work in "Ancient Future" explains higher learning concepts that can inform us of the ways of the ancients and how their teachings helped us to become knowledgeable. Wayne Chandler understands that knowledge of these ancient teachings will help us to have a vision of a different future. He is cognizant of how knowledge, that is, truth has been withheld from us. He teaches us the ancient knowledge of Djehuti or Tehuti the divinity of knowledge, wisdom, and writing; the Seven Hermetic Axioms, the principles of:

1   Mentalism
2   Correspondence
3   Vibrations
4   Polarity
5   Gender
6   Rhythm
7   Causation

In the Kemetic way of thought, knowledge itself is truth, and we call it episteme. The study of episteme knowledge is known as epistemology. One cannot have truth without knowledge and knowledge is truth. His work is based on ancient wisdoms or truths.

This work can be a foundational book for classes on the Wisdom of the ancients. In this way, such discussion will bring forth the ideas of cultural orientation, matriarchal beliefs, and the African philosophers or Sebait.

Exploring how African traditions can guide solutions to contemporary problems is critical. As we learn of the global conditions and the struggles of people across the world, we can become wiser as to how important cultural history is to evaluate what is really going on. In this way, we are developing critical thinking in the students. While we are learning of the theory of evolution, based on ideas that in ancient times humans were barbarian with no knowledge, roaming the world with no order, in mind, we can challenge such theories with evidence of how ancient people had higher learning and contemplated the meaning of life. Kemet is a starting point but not the only one. We can look at the Mayan civilization in ancient America that was literate and use the book by David Imhotep called *The First Americans were Africans*. Thus, it is possible to see that a focus on education is not a focus on war and weaponry. While a focus on education, the route to finding truth and enlightenment may be viewed in the Northern cradle culture, as a sign of weakness, naivety, uncivilization, it is possible to see that some of the knowledge that we have been prevented from knowing through cultural domination, a feature of conquest, and some of the knowledge that we have forgotten, can be useful in a Sankofa way, to think about possibilities for the future.

In the video at https://www.youtube.com/watch?v=SmtsBWvp--A&t=1231s, Ivan Van Sertima speaks of the thousands of First Nations books that were burned and the books from Africa during the time of Kemet when the library at Alexandria were burned and other libraries across the world like those of Timbuktu that were burned twice.

For instance, educators may ask the students to list Northern cradle values and Southern cradle values to show distinctions. Students may then investigate Northern cradle policies of the major institutions like, health care, economics, state governance and local governance, medicine, religions, education, sciences, environments, prisons, arts, and media.

With the cultural values of Northern and Southern cradles, the students may be divided into groups to work on a specific institution finding details of how they currently work, taking note that institutions reflect the dominant cultural values and beliefs. At this time, hierarchies based on falsehood in the belief in the inferiority of some and the superiority of others should be recognized and defined, such as media and the false stereotypical representations of phenotypes. The whole class may also be asked to look at a particular institution and bring their findings together as a cohesive collective working toward social change.

The students may discuss how the ancient principles of Maat may be applied to the same institutions and what changes could occur. In this way, students will be thinking of transforming and creating new institutions. The Imhotep Charter School in Philadelphia has a grant from the sciences, which has enabled them to find ways of cleaning water to make it drinkable.

This teaching would be Language Arts and Sociocultural Studies.

16. Medw Neter is the African Word and Hieroglyphics is the Greek Word

- **Definition:** The written language of ancient Kemet, translating to "words of the gods" or Divine words or thoughts. Early writing forms were the models that helped us to write in the languages that we use today. Writing is based on symbols. The early African symbols led to the later symbols—writings of other languages. The earliest consistent form of writing that we know of was called Mdw Ntr, by the Africans from Kemet. Mdw Ntr means divine words, Words of God.

The Mdw Ntr is metaphysical in that the images that are represented in symbolic forms are impressed upon the mind and senses. These images are reflections of the sacred sound that comes from divine speech. The mind is linked to the heart and soul so that visual impressions are being translated and transferred to the mind. The idea is that the images which formulate a message are being sent to the brain and entering consciousness. It may be said that these images are ideograms, which symbolize the sounds that they are rooted in although one cannot know the sound. The Mdw Ntr is an aspect of higher learning as one understands the complexity of humans as beings capable of processing knowledge, which is truth. One does not use the Mdw Ntr without careful thought, for when it is carved in stone or bone it is permanent, and its intention must remain true.

- **Context:**

Learning to write the Mdw Ntr is a sacred task because it is a way of understanding what our African ancestors were saying thousands of years ago. There are hardly any people in the world who can read the Mdw Ntr, the sacred writings of Kemet. Learning would be a great privilege; one can travel to the museums of the world and understand what was being said on the stone carvings. One can read the papyri and learn the ancient wisdoms of the medical papyri and learn of the operations, medications, treatments, and prescriptions for different illnesses. One can read the higher learning of the star alignments, astronomy, and astrology. Lessons in learning the Mdw Ntr will be necessary for both teacher and student. The students will learn to write regularly.

Of interest, there are other ancient writings like the writing of the Indus Valley Harrapan civilization that was conquered by the Indo-Aryans who created the Brahmin religious system, which placed them at the top of the caste system as Brahmins. As of yet, this writing has not been deciphered or translated. A lot of effort has gone into believing that it is not even a language, but only recently it has been considered a language. This denial of language is based on the reality that the Harrapan civilization was Black and African, which meant that by rights the Sudra in the caste system who are the original people who created the writing should not be at the bottom of the Brahmin hierarchy as the Indo-Aryan writing is not as ancient, and it rather spoils the logic of the falsehood to believe that those Black people at the bottom of the caste system who are not allowed to read the religious holy writings were in fact literate before their conquerors became literate.

17. Nzuri (Swahili for "Good/Beautiful")

- **Definition:** A term reflecting positive attributes and aesthetics in African cultures.

Nzuri means beautiful and good and, in this way, stays within the parameters of African beliefs that are not based on physicality but on the mind, thoughts, behaviors. Being beautiful and good is more of a reflection of the character. Beauty is portrayed in how one lives one's life. A person who shows love and compassion, care, and sensitivity toward others holds Nzuri is Nzuri. This idea is further encapsulated by the African American understanding of beauty, which reflects the same standards, "beauty is as beauty does." Standards of beauty are thus based on thoughts and behaviors, speech, and expression. Nzuri is not unlike the Kemetic word Nefer, which means the same thing. The word Nefer is associated with beauty, goodness, success, happiness, prosperity, great success, most beautiful. There is the great Queen Nefertari wife of the Per aa Ahmose from the 18th Dynasty whose beauty was known beyond Kemet. Her name lived on for over a thousand years after she entered ancestorhood. She was from Kush/Nubia and was the most revered and exalted woman in Kemet and was known as the Divinity of Resurrection.

Using this set of standards, the students may explain beauty in the terms proposed and see how beauty and goodness might be perceived in cultures across the world.

18. Chinweizu's Observations

- **Definition:** Critiques of colonialism and its impact on African societies.

Chinweizu Ibekwe's book *The West and the Rest of Us* is a classical work that those who live in the Americas and Africa should own. He studied at State University of New York in Buffalo and investigated the First Nations' history and genocide. He noted the model of the process of colonial conquest and the method used in the removal of First Nations people from their lands. His groundbreaking research identified a particular model, plan of action, theory of conquest and colonization that he argued had been applied in the Americas and was later used in the conquest and colonization of Africa. He was perhaps the first African academic or, for that matter, academic who was able to identify a model of oppression used by Europeans to successfully conquer the Americas and Africa as part of a concerted effort to colonize both the Americas and Africa. This reality led Africans to understand a more globalized analysis of important meetings taking place among Europeans to conquer the world's resources, remove any challenges to becoming the controllers of the world, and training the conquered to accept the conquest inclusive of the taking of the knowledge, wealth, minerals, raw materials, energies of the people, and using them in the interests of Europe's development and the underdevelopment of the conquered. Evidence of this type of meeting is evidenced in the meeting in Germany, at the Berlin Conference in 1885 when the whole of Africa was divided among the Europeans.

The work of Chinweizu Ibekwe has been always to speak truth and reveal anti-African movements that include the conquest and colonization of Africa by Arabs and the enslavement of Black people by Arabs as well as the corruption of governments in Africa, run by Africans, using European and Arabic governing structures to use the lands of the people to support the so-called development of everyone but African people. It is through the knowledge that Chinweizu has brought to us that we are aware of the nature of conquest and its effect on how we see and live in the world. His book on *Decolonizing the African Mind* looks toward becoming conscious of who we really are. Chinweizu is able to view those

Africans who do the work of Europeans and Arabs in continuing the colonization of Africa are betraying their own people. While it appears that in Africa, we are now independent from the colonial structures, the truth is that we are no freer than before. Now, we believe that in the advancement and superiority of the governing structures that prize materiality for the few, above the health and well-being of the majority.

There should be a discussion on Southern cradle culture and Maat the oldest set of moral principles in the world and notions of Justice. Then, there should be a discussion about Northern cradle culture and Injustice based on social hierarchies. Most importantly, the students should remember that we all have access to a cultural memory that spans the history of humanity and the time of matriarchal justice.

To make sense of the work that Chinweizu has produced, the students may be divided into two cultural groups. One cultural group is JUST and the other is UNJUST.

> One group is culturally dominant and controls the Nation with "laws" that are UNJUST.

> The other group is the conquered group living in that same UNJUST Nation state.

> The two groups, the conquerors with the dominant culture and the UNJUST laws, control the conquered group UNJUSTLY.

> The conquered group used to practice the original culture of the people, before conquest. They used to be JUST. They are being taught the UNJUST way to be and are slowly losing the memory of who they used to be.

> The dominant cultural group must seek plans to remain dominant as they fear constantly that the dominated cultural group or members of it might challenge them.

> The dominated cultural group must plan how they can challenge the dominant culture and take control without becoming UNJUST like them.

> The two groups must make ten plans each on how to maintain control or to take control.

> The solutions for both groups may take time to put into operation.

Note: This will be an important way for the students to understand the cultural transmission of values and beliefs and how dominant cultural values can influence our minds, hearts, and souls, perhaps by rewarding us with power if we do what they want or punishing us if we do not. This condition may make clearer how people make choices based on available information or knowledge. You cannot teach something that you do not know, and you cannot guide people to where you have never been, mentally. Sometimes, we are born into an UNJUST society and have never known what JUSTICE is. Sometimes, being UNJUST appears to be being JUST.

19. Trails of Tears (African Perspective), 1831–1850 Land Removal Act

- **Definition:** Reinterpreting the First Nations displacement from an Afrocentric viewpoint.

Highlighting intersections of African and Indigenous histories in America.

Applying an Afrocentric analysis of the conditions of the First Nations people of the Americas, it is necessary to recognize the African origin of humanity to understand our historical cultural relationship. Africa is the birthplace of humanity and scientifically the birthplace of the *Homo sapiens*, the first modern humans who represent humanity as we know it for at least the last 300–350,000 years ago. The First Nations people of the world were the first Diaspora of the world. These early migrations show us culturally that the first Africans were matriarchal, that is, women and men as the mothers and fathers of life and culture sought and exhibited reciprocal and complementary relationships between each other. We can still find evidence of this among differing First Nations people in the Americas as well as the Pacific islands and Australia. The chronological cultural history of the autochthonous people can reveal the similitude among the most ancient people of the world.

The First Nations people of the Americas, North, South, and Central, were cruelly conquered and their lands stolen by Europeans whether English, French, Portuguese, Spanish, or Dutch. This conquest is evidence of how Northern cradle values usurped and dominated Southern cradle values. It is a clash of cultures. Essentially, it is possible from an Afrocentric position that the First Nations people exhibited African matriarchal ways of life creating their own amazing and magnificent civilizations, for example, "Cortez observed when he entered the Aztec capital of Mexico in 1519 which at that time included parts of Texas, Colorado and California. He was amazed when he saw their temples, pyramids, palaces, floating gardens, (which were some of the most advanced agricultural systems in the world)." See Dove in *Afrikan Mothers*, pp. 91–97. There are countless stories of the greatness of First Nations' civilizations. First Nations people can be located as Africans who migrated from Africa and became the indigenous and First Nations across the world. They brought with them African matriarchal culture and settled in climates of abundance. The work of David Imhotep supports this assertion in his work *The First Americans were Africans*. The image on the cover of his book shows the paintings of the Mayans who are dark-skinned in holy attire wearing feathers as if Maatic, housed in a three-room temple on top of a pyramid. Culturally, like the Kemites, the Maya built pyramids in Mexico revealing a similitude in representation and architecture.

As a result of conquest grounded in greed and jealousy, noted in the diaries of Christopher Columbus, many nations became extinct through the genocide practiced against them. The work of Russell Thornton, *American Indian Holocaust and Survival a Population History Since 1492*, will be important for showing that genocide is not only the direct killing of a people but is related to access to resources, availability of healing methods and treatments, and the psychological impacts of trauma, for example, what people are used to growing and eating, their ancestral rituals, the shock of the conquest and the inability to procreate, and the fear of existence under tyranny, etc. The book identifies the different treatments of different nations, in the removal of nations from their lands. This removal was violent and merciless.

The perpetrators of these crimes brought unknown disease to the nations, some of which they could not recover from. This fact is a little-known reality particularly in the United States, which has been purposely negligent in explaining the First Nations genocide that took place in the construction of the Americas and, in particular, the United States, which is built upon the genocide of the First Nations people in North America, the Caribbean, and South America. Jan Carew writes of the character of Christopher Columbus who first landed in Ayiti or Haiti, the home of the Taino people, also known as Cristobel Colon, and how he debases women and the murders he committed with his own hands, in his book *The Rape of Paradise*. Although it is known that the First Nations people of Brazil are still fighting for their lands and life in the forests, against the Portuguese government and militia trained to take the lands and kill the people, and burn the forests where the people exist with nature and the animals, there is no foreign policy to bring this continuing holocaust to either the mind or to an end. At this moment, Guajajara Guardians of the Forest in Brazil and other indigenous nations who are defending their lands, live in terror and danger as they protect their lands against the loggers and mining companies clearing lands.

The "trail of tears" is defined by the context of the general First Nations' holocaust. It has been said that there were many "trails of tears" relating to land clearance and the deaths of the people taken off their lands and taken to "Indian Lands." Essentially, no matter what treaties and laws were made between the First Nations people, classified as red, the Europeans, classified as white, broke them. One understands this situation within the context of the clash of cultural beliefs. First Nations people had produced amazing civilizations and writing systems although many were destroyed through the burning of books by religious zealots like Cardinal Ximenes Grand Inquisitor of Spain in the early 1500s considered works of the devil. Writing itself and its meaning to First Nations people was grounded in the sacred notions of ancient writings like the Mdw Ntr.

The Popol Vu is the Mayan book of the Dawn of Life and the Glories of Gods and Kings. It is one of the Mayan books defining the creation of the world. In the introduction, the author is explaining the Mayan civilization as rooted in the Olmec civilization flowering on the Gulf coastal plain of Veracruz and Tabasco by about 1200 BCE. The translator, Dennis Tedlock, speaks of hieroglyphics carved in stone and stucco, painted on pottery and plaster and inked on longs strips of paper that were folded like screens to make books. The knowledge of this ancient writing would perhaps lead the First Nations people to trust the writing of contracts and treaties in that they were expected to portray sacred or divine thoughts of truth.

Culturally, this was far from the experience of Europeans and Northern cradle values, which were built upon the lies and beliefs in the inferiority of women particularly Black, and the inferiority of humans particularly Black. This was the nature of the conquest, the belief in the authority of the superior white based on strength grounded in deadly weapons to take the lands of lesser people and control their lives and resources. We can go back historically to the Indo-Aryan roots of these beliefs regarding the conquest of the Indus Valley civilization. The First Nations people were deemed the red people and lower down in the scale of superiority. The reality for First Nations people as phenotypes was that they began as dark skin classical African types, and many Black nations like the Seminole, still existed during the time that their lands were being forcibly stolen. There are still Black First Nations people today. It has been said that after enslavement, the movement of enslaved Black Africans leaving the plantation in the South migrating to the North for paid work was inclusive of countless Black First Nations people who joined their sisters and brothers, undetectable from those who had been enslaved. The fight for the lands was ongoing and culturally First Nations people had to make choices of whether to take the assimilationist, acculturationist, or traditionalist route toward a kind of freedom from death. This has been the case in all colonizing and colonized countries, the conquered must learn and take on the beliefs and values of the conquerors.

In Africa, the North is conquered by the Arabs. Thus, these African countries speak Arabic. The South is conquered by Europeans and the languages of Portuguese, French, English, Belgium, Italian, and Dutch are spoken as the dominant language. All "educational" institutions teach these languages and uphold the theories of the supposed inferiority of conquered. None were free from terror then and now.

Perhaps the most famous of those who traveled the "trail of tears" were the so-called five "civilized nations" the Seminoles, Cherokees, Choctaws, Creeks, and Chickasaws who took the Europeanization route, practiced Northern cradle beliefs, became Christianized, married European women and men and developed English-speaking schools. They even owned enslaved Africans, grew cotton, had guns, and supported the Southern racists. Whether they were cruel to Africans or to some extent harbored Africans is not fully known. There was certainly a relationship between

African people running away from enslavement and finding refuge with First Nations people. These stories are becoming known. Those who crossed the boundaries of race were considered dangerous. The attempts to cause trouble among perceived races was always preferred in terms of the conquerors' control. The civilized nations fared no better than those who took the traditionalist route to maintain their cultural beliefs and values. The belief in races has been fundamental to the justification of conquest. There is only one human race; thus, the trick has been to define phenotypes as races, and in this way, it has been possible to separate and control people, as it was then for the red people and later the Black people. After settling and becoming sedentary, the so-called "civilized nations" were then uprooted from their homes forced to travel miles from their homelands as part of land clearance, based upon the Indian Removal Act that took place from 1831 to 1850. Their lands would yield 25 million acres of land to the European settlement plan. President Andrew Jackson carried out the brutal removal of the people from their lands. They were taken from the South to what was deemed Indian Territory, now called Oklahoma. Countless thousands of First Nations people died on this journey and thousands on other trails of tears. The Creek trail of tears lost over 8,000 Creeks, more than half of those Creek forced to leave their lands (https://www.youtube.com/watch?v=CM8PcTIRbDk).

CONCLUSION: CULTURE AND SOCIETY

In Kemet, the practice of Maat was considered a moral necessity for individuals in all walks of life to practice so that it manifested in the public arena. Maat was foundational for governing, and thus, there was consideration and care for the unfortunate, vulnerable, poor, elderly, hungry, thirsty, etc. Maaticity is a philosophical position emphasizing the practice of Maat in the process of becoming human in a relational sense, where we seek to relate to others, the environment, and the metaphysical world (Asante & Dove, 2021).

Culture impacts us, and negative culture transforms human thoughts and behaviors. An objective is to bring to light cultural distinctions as proposed and theorized by Cheikh Anta Diop. Essentially, the two cradles are differentiated by the positioning of the woman as the potential mother.

The original culture developed in Africa and is known as African matriarchy positions women and men as seeking and acquiring complementary relations with each other, which are reflected in the institutions that govern the practices of people in all walks of life from the family, health care, education, government, politics, economics, religion, spiritual systems, sciences, etc. This balanced and reciprocal relations between the mother and father ultimately led to the development of Maat, the oldest set of moral principles that we know of. They are Justice, Truth, Righteousness, Reciprocity, Harmony, Balance, and Order. These principles were reproduced in all the institutions that uplift the culture and character of a people based on respect. This culture was born 350,000 years ago by the first modern humans, *Homo sapiens*, our Black African ancestors who gave life to humanity.

The second culture was created perhaps 3 to 4,000 years ago after some people left Africa 60 to 70,000 years ago and populated the world as the First Nations people of the world. Those missing years are being investigated by Afrocentric researchers who believe in the wisdom, knowledge, intelligence of the early people who built ancient civilizations, and left their symbols and artifacts behind that let us know of their consciousness that has provided evidence that these people practiced African matriarchal values, although many phenotypes have changed. Phenotypical differences should be rejoiced and loved. There is an understanding in this guide that the construction of the falsehood of patriarchy and race led to the dislocation of humanity in the belief that differences equate to species that can never come together in peace and that war is the method to resolve the world's problems based on the inhumane practices of humans who no longer know their higher selves and have resorted to barbarism. The concept of barbarism shows us how far away we have come from civilization. Civilization begins with the reciprocity and complementarity between women and men: the mothers and fathers of life and culture.

African matriarchy set the terms for civilization. An objective of this guide is to show that it is possible for humanity to become culturally oriented in ancient principles of civilization that have been transmitted over centuries. The awakening of our cultural memory in this barbarian time, as the wars in Congo, Sudan (Kush/Nubia), Yemen, Palestine, etc. continue, is based on the knowledge—truth that we must accrue. These and other wars are grounded in land acquisitions, the search for mineral wealth based on the fact that some have the right to ownership regardless of borders and boundaries. Beneath notions of patriarchy and race, lie the belief in the "survival of the fittest" thus those whose weapons are most powerful will decide who deserves to live or die as they have done for hundreds of years during which time lands and wealth of any people have been taken and usurped without any moral principles. Morality today is a dirty word, and yet we humans once lived by them. There has been an attempt to show that we are free to learn and join a cultural orientation. We have the real choice of two major cultures recognizing that there are thousands of variations. The fundamental differences lie in the positioning of the woman and man as the creators of life and culture. African matriarchy, the oldest culture of civilization, is the journey toward decolonizing our minds and seeing the light of our potential. The journey of enlightenment is an educational process and intergenerational, and it is cultural and of the heart and soul. In this way, we can embrace values and beliefs that can sustain life from the humans to the plants and animals and all of nature in the way that our foremothers and fathers did and some still do, most of whom are represented by our First Nations people across the world who are under threat of extinction. They are the wisdom keepers, and we must learn to value them to save humanity. We have the power as the privileged to teach and learn the reality of our existence. The greatest accomplishments in the sciences and thoughts were born in African matriarchal societies. It is not to be a feminist to love and strive for African matriarchy. It is not to betray our "races" to condone white supremacy and love all phenotypes. It is not to be a romantic to want our dislocation from each other to be healed. It is within our reach to begin the process of dismantling falsehoods and developing new thoughts on how to proceed. The guide is to first uncover the barbarism that we have grown to rely on and open our minds to the potential of humanity outside of the limitations of patriarchy and race, the cultural foundations of aggression, lies, hypocrisy, hatred, murder, genocide, jealousy, individualism, materialism, and the blights that live in our minds to destroy. Afrocentricity is not a religion.

As professor Molefi Kete Asante (2007) stated:

> Afrocentricity is an intellectual idea that suggests that African people must be viewed and must view themselves as agents in the historical process ... my political ideology is my own business. What does it matter that I am a Black Nationalist, Marxist, Democrat, Republican, Socialist or Anarchist? My religious faith is my business. What does it matter that I am an atheist, Christian, Jew, Yoruba, Muslim or Shintoist? Afrocentricity as a way of interpreting reality begins with the idea that it is teachable and accessible to anyone who cares to learn it ... the Afrocentrist will teach anyone how to become a scholar who begins the study of African people and African phenomena from the standpoint of Africans as subjects rather than objects of history. (p. 22)

My hope is that this guide provides an overview of some of the contradictions that arise when using patriarchy and race as theoretical models to create "educational" curriculum syllabi and critical thoughts. Lies should not be the basis of "education" as they fly in the face of the concept and philosophy of a true education, which is the journey to enlightenment. Our cultural orientation is founded on truth or lies, and only we can make that choice.

References

ABC News (Australia). (2011, September 23). *Aboriginal DNA provides human migration clues* [Video]. YouTube. https://www.youtube.com/watch?v=2qlTQorAigA

African History Fountain. (2023, July 16). *The Shang connection: Did this Nigerian tribe start Chinese civilization?* [Video]. YouTube. https://www.youtube.com/watch?v=PIYqtI3Ik30

Ambedkar, B. R. (2022[1936]). *Annihilation of Caste, with a reply to Mahatma.* Kalpaz Publications.

American Council of Learned Societies. (1999). *American national biography.* Oxford University Press.

Asante, M. K. (1988). *Afrocentricity.* Africa World Press.

Asante, M. K. (1998). *The Afrocentric idea, revised and expanded edition.* Temple University Press.

Asante, M. K. (2000). *The Egyptian philosophers: Ancient African voices from Imhotep to Akhenaten.* African American Images.

Asante, M. K. (2003). *Afrocentricity: The theory of social change* (Revised and expanded). African American Images.

Asante, M. K. (2007). *An Afrocentric manifesto.* Polity Press.

Asante, M. K. (2017). *Revolutionary pedagogy: Primer for teachers of Black children.* Universal Write Publications.

Asante, M. K., & Dove, N. (2021). *Being human being.* Universal Write Publications.

Birnbaum, L. C. (2001). Dark mother: *African origins and godmothers.* Authors Choice Press.

Black Journals. (2023, July 23). *DNA confirms Chinese are direct Africa descendants* [Video]. YouTube. https://www.youtube.com/watch?v=su9WTof7k5s

Browder, A. (1992). *Nile Valley contributions to civilization: Exploding the myths.* The Institute of Karmic Guidance.

Burt, C. (1961). *The backward child* (5th ed.). University of London Press.

Busby, M. (1992). *Daughters of Africa: An international anthology of words and writings by women of African descent from the ancient Egyptian to the present.* Ballantine Books.

Carew, J. (1994). *Rape of paradise: Columbus and the birth of racism in the Americas*. A & B Publishers.

Centers for Disease Control (CDC). (2024a). Births: Final data for 2022. *National Vital Statistics Reports, 73*(2), 1–19. https://www.cdc.gov/nchs/data/nvsr/nvsr73/nvsr73-05.pdf

Centers for Disease Control (CDC). (2024b). Maternal mortality rates in the United States, 2022. *National Center for Health Statistics* (pp. 1–6). https://www.cdc.gov/nchs/data/hestat/maternal-mortality/2022/maternal-mortality-rates-2022.pdf

Chandler, W. (1999). *Ancient future: The teachings and prophetic wisdom of the seven hermetic laws of ancient Egypt*. Black Classic Press.

Chinweizu, I. (1975). *The west and the rest of us, White predators, Black slavers and the African elite*. Vintage Books.

Churchill, W., & Vander Wall, J. (1990). *Agents of repression*. South End Press.

Coard, B. (1971). *How the West Indian child is made educationally sub-normal in the British school system*. New Beacon Books.

de Volney, C. F. (1991[1791]). *The ruins of empires*. Black Classic Press.

Diop, C. A. (1989). *The cultural unity of Black Africa: The domains of matriarchy and patriarchy in classical antiquity*. Karnak House.

Diop, C. A. (1991a). *Civilization or barbarism: An authentic anthropology*. Lawrence Hill.

Diop, C. A. (1991b). *The African origin of civilization: Myth or reality*. Lawrence Hill Books.

Diop, C. A. (1996). *Toward the African renaissance*. Karnak House.

Diop, C. A., Leclant, J., Obenga, T., & Vercoutter, J. (1997). *The peopling of ancient Egypt & the deciphering of the Meroitic script*. Karnak House.

Dove, N. (1993). *Racism and resistance in the schooling of Afrikans* [Unpublished PhD Dissertation]. American Studies, State University of New York at Buffalo.

Dove, N. (1995). An African-centered critique of Marx's logic. *The Western Journal of Black Studies, 19*(4), 260–271.

Dove, N. (1998a). African womanism as Afrocentric theory. *Journal of Black Studies, 28*(5), 515–539.

Dove, N. (1998b). *Afrikan mothers, bearers of culture, makers of social change*. SUNY Press.

Dove, N. (2002). Defining a mother-centered matrix to analyze the status of women. *Journal of Black Studies, 33*(1), 3–24.

Dove, N. (2015). Cultural identity. In M. Shujaa & K. Shujaa (Eds.), *The encyclopedia of African cultural heritage in North America* (pp. 110–112). Sage.

Dove, N. (2018). Race revisited, against a cultural construction bearing significant implications. *International Journal of African Renaissance Studies,*

Multi-Inter and Transdisciplinary, 13(2), 129–143. https://doi.org/10.1080/1 8186874.2018.1538703

Dove, N. (2021). *The Afrocentric school [a blueprint].* Universal Write Publications.

Dove, N. (2025). Re-defining African womanism as Afrocentric theory: Voicing Maat. In V. Okafor (Ed.), *Afrocology: Afrocentricity & the transdisciplinary legacy of Diopian epistemology* (Chapter 9). Taylor & Francis.

DeGruy, J. (2017). *Post-traumatic slave syndrome: Americas legacy of enduring injury and healing.* Joy DeGruy Publications.

Ephirim-Donkor, A. (1997). *African spirituality, on becoming ancestors.* African World Press.

Ephirim-Donkor, A. (2021). *African spirituality, on becoming ancestors* (3rd ed.). Hamilton Books.

Finch III, C. (2023). *Nile Valley civilization: A 10,000-year history.* Khenti, Inc.

François, M. (2019, May 7). It's not just Cambridge University—all of Britain benefited from slavery. *The Guardian.* https://www.theguardian.com/ commentisfree/2019/may/07/cambridge-university-britain-slavery

Goodwin, M. (2020a). *Policing the womb: Invisible women and the criminalization of motherhood.* Cambridge University Press.

Goodwin, M. (2020b). The new Jane Crow: Women's mass incarceration. *Just Security.* https://www.justsecurity.org/71509/the-new-jane-crow-womens-mass-incarceration/#:~:text=If%20Pauli%20Murray%20were%20alive,and%20 the%20criminal%20justice%20system

Gould, S. J. (1981). *The mismeasure of man.* Penguin Books Canada.

Grimaldi Man. (n.d.). *Wikipedia.* Retrieved March 20, 2024, from https:// en.wikipedia.org/wiki/Grimaldi_man

Hegel, G. W. (1975). *George Wilhelm Friedrich Hegel, lectures on the philosophy of world history: Reason in history* (H. B. Nisbet, Trans.). Cambridge University Press.

Herskovits, M. (1990[1941]). *The myth of the Negro past.* Beacon Press.

Hill, L. (2009). *The book of negroes.* Harper Collins Publishers.

Hilliard, III, A. G. (2014, December 29). *Free your mind: return to the source.* 6:00. [video] YouTube. https://www.youtube.com/watch?=659s.

Hilliard, III, A. G., Willams, L., & Damali, N. (1987). *The teachings of Ptah Hotep: The oldest book in the world.* Blackwood Press & Company.

Holloway, J. (1991). *Africanisms in American Culture.* Indiana University Press.

Howitt, D., & Owusu-Bempah, J. (1994). *The racism of psychology, time for change.* Harvester/Wheatsheaf.

Hoyert, D. L. (2023). Maternal mortality rates in the United States, 2021. *NCHS Health E-Stats.* https://doi.org/10.15620/cdc:124678

Imhotep, D. (2021). *The first Americans were Africans: Expounded and revised* (2nd ed.). Self-published.

Isaacson, R. (2002, August 27). Last exit from the Kalahari: The slow genocide of the Bushmen/San. *Open Democracy.* https://www.opendemocracy.net/en/article_267jsp/

James, G. M. (1989). *Stolen legacy* (Republished). United Brothers Communications Systems.

Jok, M. (2001). *War and slavery in Sudan.* University of Pennsylvania Press.

Karenga, M. (1984). *Selections from the Husia, sacred wisdoms of ancient Egypt.* University of Sankore Press.

Karenga, M. (2006). *Maat, the moral ideal in ancient Egypt: A study of classical African ethics.* University of Sankore Press.

Kessler, D. (1996). *The Falashas: A short history of the Ethiopian Jews.* Frank Cass & Co. Ltd.

King, J. E. (1991). Dysconscious racism: Ideology, identity, and the miseducation of teachers. *Journal of Negro Education, 60*(2), 133–146.

Knowles, R. (2020, February 18). Rising rate of Aboriginal children in out-of-home care. *National Indigenous Times.* https://nit.com.au/18-02-2020/388/rising-rate-of-aboriginal-children-in-out-of-home-care

Lee, D. (2007). *Penguin classics, Plato, the republic.* Penguin Books Ltd.

Leinster-Mackay, D. (1988). The nineteenth century English preparatory school: Cradle and creche of empire? In J. A. Mangan (Ed.), *Benefits bestowed* (pp. 56–76). Manchester University Press.

Lesko, B. (1996). *The remarkable women of ancient Egypt.* B. & C. Scribe Publications.

Lewis, R. (Ed.). (2012). *William Petty on the order of nature: An unpublished manuscript treatise.* Medieval and Renaissance Texts and Studies 399. Arizona Center for Medieval and Renaissance Studies.

Lichtheim, M. (1975). *Ancient Egyptian Literature Vol I: the Old and Middle Kingdoms.* University of California Press.

Lindqvist, S. (1996). *Exterminate all the Brutes: One man's odyssey into the heart of darkness and the origins of European genocide.* The New Press.

MacRitchie, D. (1991). *Ancient and modern Britons: A retrospect.* Pine Hill Press, Inc.

Maglangbayan, S., & Moore, C. (1976). Interview with foreign minister Ben Tanggahma. *Black Books Bulletin, 4*(2).

Malaspinas, A.-S., Westaway, M. C., Muller, C., Sousa, V. C., Lao, O., Alves, I., Bergström, A., Athanasiadis, G., Cheng, J. Y., Crawford, J. E., Heupink, T. H., Macholdt, E., Peischl, S., Rasmussen, S., Schiffels, S., Subramanian, S.,

Wright, J. L., Albrechtsen, A., Barbieri, C., ... Willerslev, E. (2016). A genomic history of Aboriginal Australia. *Nature, 538*, 207–214. https://www.nature.com/articles/nature18299

McBride, J. (2006). *The color of water: A Black man's tribute to his White mother*. Riverhead Books.

McGhee, C. J. (2022). *19 White men who admitted there were indigenous Black people in the Americas*. Self-published.

Monteiro-Ferreira, A. (2014). *The demise of the inhuman, Afrocentricity, modernism and post modernism*. SUNY Press.

Muhammad Ali refuses to fight in Vietnam (1967). (n.d.). *alphahistory*. https://alphahistory.com/vietnamwar/muhammad-ali-refuses-to-fight-1967/

NBC News. (2022, November 16). *The reckoning: Native American boarding schools' painful history unearthed* [Video]. YouTube. https://www.youtube.com/watch?v=pcAZsf96d3U

Nehusi, K. (2016). *Libation*. University Press of America.

Nobles, W. (2006). *Seeking the Sakhu: Foundational writings for an African psychology*. Third World Press.

Okafor, V. O. (1991). Diop and the African origin of civilization: An Afrocentric analysis. *Journal of Black Studies, 22*(2), 252–268.

Olusoga, D. (2021). *Black and British: A forgotten history*. Pan Books.

Online Media TV. (2018, August 10). *Members of the Khoisan community weigh in on the land debate and their culture* [Video]. YouTube. https://www.youtube.com/watch?v=w1ZkIdgbj5g

Probyn-Rapsey, F. (2013). *Made to matter: White fathers, stolen generations*. Sydney University Press.

Quakers and Slavery. (n.d.). *Borthwick Institute for Archives*. https://www.york.ac.uk/borthwick/holdings/research-guides/race/quakers-and-slavery/#:~:text=The%20Society%20of%20Friends%20(known,in%20the%20Anti%2DSlavery%20Society

Rajshekar, V. T. (1987). *Dalit: The Black untouchables of India*. Clarity Press.

Reséndez, A. (2017). *The other slavery: The uncovered story of Indian enslavement in America*. Houghton Mifflin Harcourt.

RetroGrading w/Phoenix*X. (2017, April 1). *The Irish sugar slaves of Barbados* [Video]. YouTube. https://www.youtube.com/watch?v=kY4rDnb11bY

Rich, P. J. (1988). Public school freemasonry in the empire: Mafia of the mediocre. In J. A. Mangan (Ed.), *Benefits bestowed* (pp. 174–193). Manchester University Press.

Roberts, A. (2021). *The last king of America: The misunderstood reign of George III*. Viking.

Robinson, C. (1983). *Black Marxism: The making of the Black radical tradition.* Zed Press.

Rosenthal, R., & Jacobson, L. (1968). *Pygmalion in the classroom: Teacher expectation and student intellectual development.* Holt, Rinehart & Winston.

SBC News. (2023, June 6). *Streets of Philadelphia, Kensington Ave documentary, May 25–26, 2023* [Video]. YouTube. https://www.youtube.com/watch?v=v2Y43qilPiU

Shevoroshkin, V. V. (1990). The mother tongue: How linguists have reconstructed the ancestor of all living languages. *The Sciences, 30*(3), 20–27.

Shujaa, M. (1998). *Too much schooling, too little education: A paradox of Black life in white societies.* Africa World Press.

Simpson, T. (2023, December 5). *How did South African Apartheid happen, and how did it finally end?* [Video]. YouTube. https://www.youtube.com/watch?v=ke4kVFycpYY

Smith, S., & Ellis, K. (2017, September 4). *Shackled legacy: History shows slavery helped build many U.S. colleges and universities.* https://www.apmreports.org/episode/2017/09/04/shackled-legacy

The African Origins of China: The Genographic Project. (2023, May 9). *Afro culture blog.* https://afrocultureblog.over-blog.com/2023/05/the-african-origins-of-china-the-genographic-project.html

Spencer, H. Spencer. (2017 [1864]). *The principles of biology* (Vol. 1). HardPress.

Thornton, R. (1987). *American Indian holocaust and survival: A population history since 1492.* University of Oklahoma Press.

Tise, E. L. (1987)). *Proslavery: A history of the defense of slavery in America 1701–1840.* University of Georgia Press.

Tshaka, O. (1995). *Return to the African mother principle of male and female equality* (Vol 1). Pan Afrikan Publishers.

Uluru Statement from the Heart. (2017). *The Uluru statement.* https://ulurustatement.org/the-statement/view-the-statement/

Van Sertima, I., & Rashidi, R. (Eds.). (1988). *African presence in early Asia.* Transaction Publishers.

Walker, R. (2006). *When we ruled: The ancient and medieval history of black civilisations.* Every Generation Media.

Williams, C. (1987). *The destruction of Black civilization.* Third World Press.

Woodson, C. G. (1933a). *The education of the Negro.* Hakim Publications.

Woodson, C. G. (1933b). *The miseduction of the Negro.* Chump Change Edition.

Yellen, J. E., Brooks, A. S., Cornelissen, E., Mehlman, M. J., & Stewart, K. (1995). A middle stone age worked bone industry from Katanda, Upper Semliki Valley, Zaire. *Science, 268*(5210), 553–556.

Yunkaporta, T. (2019). Sand talk. In: *How indigenous thinking can save the world.* The Text Publishing Company.

Index

domination of women, 173
European academic interpretation, 132
and race, 189, 190
Peck, Raoul, 14n7
Pentateuch, version of *Book of Coming Forth by Day*, 141
Pepi I, 6th Dynasty ruler, 138
Peres, Shimon, 43–44
permanence in writing (stone/bone), 179
Persians, 19, 38, 44, 57, 65, 94–95
Petrie, Flinders, 148
Petty, William, 55
Pharaoh, 17
phenotypes, 114, 121, 126, 146, 173, 188
Philadelphus, 94
Philippines, 86
philosophy and logic, 147
Phoenicians, 140
Piaget, Jean, 2
Plato, 119
polygenesis, 15, 158
Portuguese colonization (Brazil), 185
Portuguese monopoly, 11n3
Pratt, Richard, 24
prejudices, 146
pre-Kemet, 137
Prince Albert I, 77
Princess Diana, 10
Probyn-Rapsey, Fiona, 80
"Pro-slavery" movement, 28
pseudo-sciences, 15, 55, 60–61, 123
psychology, cultural identity and, 53, 58–59
Ptahhotep, 109, 111, 118, 153
Ptolemaic Dynasty, founded by Ptolemy I, 142
Ptolemy II Philadelphus, 148
public education, aim of, 64
Pygmalion effect, 125
Pyramid age, 138
pyramids, 47, 71–73
Pythagoras, 148–149

The Quakers, 28, 103

race and racism, 5–6, 14, 103, 113, 123, 167
basis for colonial decision-making, 117
as belief, 27
construction of, 18
as cultural and social construct, 10, 121, 126, 176
defining, 121
discourse, 44
exclusion of, 22
falsehood of, 55, 81
identity, 126–127

impact on Black and white lives, 124
learning, pro-Black or anti-Black values, 125–126
as mental illness, 16
paradigm, 14, 17, 21, 64, 81, 116, 117, 125
and patriarchy, 21, 91–92, 131
philosophy, 134
pseudo-sciences in, 55
racial boundaries, 125
theory, 15, 25–26, 38, 44–45
translation and, 77
unifying factor for humanity, 125
used in educational books, 126
See also white supremacy
Ragland, Dora, 10
Rameses II, 140
Rameses III, 56, 140
Ramsey, Allan, 10
The Rape of Paradise (Carew), 185
relationships (*abantu* concept), 176
religion, cultural identity and, 59–61
religious racialized hierarchy (caste origins), 129
remembering history process, 90
Republic (Plato), 119
restorative justice, 145
rhetoric, 154
Rig Veda, 60
rites of passage, teaching responsibilities to nations, 161
rock paintings, 93
Romans, 20, 38–39, 57, 65, 94–97
Rosetta Stone, Ptolemy IV decree, 142
Rousseau, Jean-Jacques, 55
Ruins of Empires (de Volney), 39
Russian–Ukrainian war, 125

"Sankofa" (Gerima), 164
Sankofa, 90, 107n3, 164, 178
Schock, Robert, 147
Seba and Sebait (wise and wisdom-teaching), 118, 168–171, 178
sebait, 118
Second Intermediate Period, Dynasties 13–17, nomadic invasion, 139
seeking the Sakhu concept, 53, 53n1
Sekhmet, 97, 131
self, knowledge of, 152
Seminoles, 186
Semite, 56
Semliki harpoon tip, 111
Septuagint, Greek version of Hebrew scriptures, 142
Seshat, 109, 133, 153–156
Set, 130

Author Biography

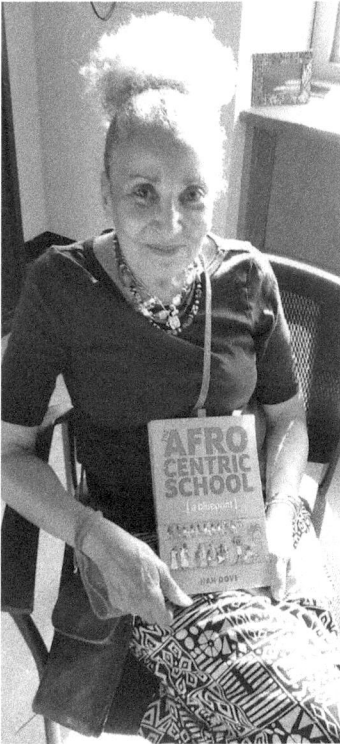

Dr Nah Dove is a proud mother, grandmother, and great-grandmother. She has lived in Ghana, Nigeria, Canada, the US, and the UK. She graduated with a PhD from the State University of New York, Buffalo, with a focus on African Cultural orientation, First Nations Studies Black Women's Studies, African American Studies and Education. Nah Dove is an African Womanist and has written articles, book chapters, encyclopedic entries, and three books: *African Mothers: Bearers of Culture, Makers of Social Change* (1998), *The Afrocentric School [a blueprint]* (2021), and co-authored *Being Human Being: Transforming the Race Discourse* (2021) with Dr Molefi Kete Asante. She has a forthcoming title, TEACHING TEACHERS, with Universal Write Publications. Nah Dove's accomplishments include her involvement in promoting the development of African-centered/Afrocentric schools in the UK, Brazil, and US. Dr Nah Dove is an Assistant Professor of Africology at Temple University with a focus on African Culture, African/Black Women as potential mothers, Afronographic research methods, and Africological episteme.

www.ingramcontent.com/pod-product-compliance
Lightning Source LLC
Chambersburg PA
CBHW052112030426
42335CB00025B/2943